# BLUE ATTITUDES

*is*

*Presented to:*

_____

*Presented from:*

_____

*Date:*

_____

*Occasion:*

_____

# BLUE

## ATTITUDES

MANY BLESSINGS!

Cover Design / Interior Layout:
Lane Davis of Monroe, LA
www.facebook.com/lanedavis.designer
gabrieldesignworks@gmail.com

*To the men and women of law enforcement, who proudly and courageously wear the uniform and badge, may God keep you safe.*

*To the spouses and families of those who are called to serve in law enforcement, may God give you peace.*

# CONTENTS

# FOREWORD

When Matt began writing this book, I truly wondered if he had lost his mind. I was in the middle of writing a dissertation and felt like writing was a chore that served little purpose. He hated writing, and sometimes the idea of editing his work felt like a chore for me. Over time, though, the process became beautiful.

As I watched him struggle with what to say and become invigorated by his new thoughts, I realized that what he was writing was more than some idealistic exercise. He was writing to himself. He was learning how to meld his Christian beliefs with a job that is thankless and trying. Bible study became an integral part of his every day walk.

Matt didn't just write a book, he began to open up parts of himself that had never been exposed. He began by talking about events, but ended up talking about the way he felt about his life, his job, and his calling. He started to share parts of himself with me that were new. I didn't know that after more than a decade together there were still so many parts of him that I hadn't seen. He began opening up about brutal realities that he had lived. He shared raw emotion and painful memories. Reading the book required remembering painful times in our marriage; we recounted times when we were not sure that we would make it. Talking about the emptiness he felt made me remember the emptiness I felt as we drifted in a life without a Savior. It was painful but also beautiful because we could see so clearly how far God had brought us.

It wasn't just in the stories about our relationship that we felt an emotional burden, but also in talking about Matt's experiences with death. Reading how he felt triggered memories of helplessness in me. I felt as if I couldn't keep him safe at work and could not relieve his sadness when he returned home. Again, discussing the pain and difficulty demonstrated how loving our God is. It was apparent that God had his hand on us as we walked through treacherous times. We were never alone. He carried us through the tough times and sent messengers to retrieve us when we were lost.

The emotional and spiritual journey softened Matt. He became softer with his kids and with me. He began really thinking about people he arrested as just that, PEOPLE. They weren't "bad guys" anymore. They were souls who were lost and in need of a Savior. He stopped seeing the world as an ugly, hopeless place and started seeing the beauty of salvation. When he REALLY saw it, he wanted nothing more than to share that beauty with everyone around him. This book helped him to have a better understanding of salvation and begin developing a truly fulfilling relationship with his Savior, Jesus Christ.

I hope that as you read this book, you are also renewed and challenged to become who Christ wants you to be in your personal and professional life.

*Candi L. Hill*

*I offer my thanks and praise to God for making this book possible. It was through His inspiration and guidance that this vision became a reality.*

*Thanks to my loving and beautiful wife, Candi, for providing me with encouragement and support.*

*For I know the plans I have for you"—this is the Lord's declaration—"plans for your welfare, not for disaster, to give you a future and a hope.*
Jeremiah 29:11 (HCSB)

# INTRODUCTION

As a child, I knew that I wanted to work in law enforcement. I was always fascinated by television shows like Walker Texas Ranger, Cops, T.J. Hooker, and even Inspector Gadget where, in the end, the good guys always won. I loved watching officers who were driving in high speed chases, finding dope and stolen cars, and then, victoriously arresting the bad guys. This excited me and I was eager to get in on the thrill of helping the good guys win the fight. This need to help the good guys win was always a part of me, which is evident by the fact that in elementary school, I decided that I should be the bus monitor. So, without being asked, I kept a list of the names of people on the school bus who were breaking the "rules."

I always knew that being a police officer was for me. There was never any doubt about what I wanted to be when I grew up. My childhood interests were obvious to everyone. There is even picture evidence that I ALWAYS wanted to be a police officer. I recently found a picture of me wearing a plastic badge on my shirt and a holster that held a cap gun around my waist. Growing up, I thought that I was simply interested in working in law enforcement, but later I realized that it was more than an interest, it was a calling.

Unlike law enforcement, Christianity is somewhat new to me. For that matter, I didn't decide to accept Jesus Christ as my Savior until 2008. The journey is new and I still have a long way to go, but as I've begun to grow in my faith, my beliefs about my interest in law enforcement have changed dramatically. Viewing the world through the lens of God's Word has challenged me to think differently about who I am and what I do. For example, in the Old Testament, the Israelites were God's chosen people and He chose them to live out His special purpose. After reading through the Bible, I've found over and over again, that God calls people according to His purpose. I believe that God calls all Christians to fulfill some sort of purpose. Paul writes to the Romans, "We know that all things work together for the good of those who love God: those who are called according to His purpose". Romans 8:28 (HCSB).

My childhood interest may have simply been me recognizing my calling, without knowing that's what I was doing. Is it possible that God started molding me from the womb? Jeremiah wrote, "I chose you before I formed you in the womb; I set you apart before you were born. I appointed you a prophet to the nations." Jeremiah 1:5 (HCSB) Here, Jeremiah was writing what he was told by God. How awesome is that? God was planning our lives before the womb. What if God planned for me to be an officer before the womb? What if He appointed me to be a police officer, to fulfill a special purpose, before my parents knew that I would exist? Now, that is amazing!

So maybe we were called to service by God. I can't imagine any other good reason, except that I was called by God, why I, being a rational person, would choose a profession that requires me to go into dark buildings without knowing what dangers awaited, miss birthdays and other family events, or get out of bed in the middle of the night to help with relief efforts after a severe storm.

Being a police officer means having authority, and that authority is given to me by God. In Romans 13:1, HCSB, Paul says, "Everyone must submit to the governing authorities, for there is no authority except from God, and those that exist are instituted by God." It isn't my choice to have authority. The choice is God's. So, I believe that I didn't choose to be a police officer, but that I was called into the profession by God, and the authority I have is a God-granted privilege that I must not abuse. I am in this profession to serve His purpose, not mine.

The word "Beatitude" means supreme blessedness or exalted happiness[1]. The most commonly recognized Beatitudes are from the Sermon on the Mount, which is the teaching given by Jesus in Matthew Chapters 5-7 where

He gives Christian ideals that focus on love in the form of conditions and results[2]. These will be the primary focus of this book. There are, however, other Beatitudes found in the Bible, from Psalms to Revelation, and some of them will be addressed as well.

After reading through the Beatitudes given by Jesus in the Sermon on the Mount, I began to think about how to apply those principles to my job as a police officer. At that moment, thanks to my smarter-than-me wife, the term "Blueattitude" was born. What is a Blueattitude? Well, it is a play on words, conceived by blending the term "Blue" as it commonly identifies police officers and "Beatitudes". I want the term "Blueattitude" to be representative of how the Beatitudes apply to me and my profession, but I also want it to be a reminder of how I actually apply them to being a cop.

The information in this book is meant to be a guide, based upon God's Word, for law enforcement officers on how to conduct themselves according to the Beatitudes of the Bible. It's full of Scripture and on-the-job stories about various times during my career. I'm including stories where I feel like I met the expectations of Jesus, and examples of times when I failed to rise to the occasion. None of the stories are meant to suggest that I've got it all figured out. Believe me, I don't. They are also not meant to boast or brag on me. I'm a Christian police officer writing this book to myself as motivation and guidance to be a man whose words and actions exemplify the love of God.

Writing this book has been a great learning experience because not only was it a good Bible study, but I really had to learn to examine myself and be honest about admitting the times when I failed and didn't represent Christ.

*But He answered, "It is written: Man must not live on bread alone but on every word that comes from the mouth of God."*
Matthew 4:4 (HCSB)

# IT'S ALL HIS

## CHAPTER 1

*"Blessed are the poor in spirit, for theirs is the Kingdom of Heaven."*
Matthew 5:3 (WEB)

"I quit! I'm done! I give up! I just can't do it!" I sometimes feel this way when I'm overwhelmed, when I can't do something by myself, or when I just can't seem to reach my goal. Then the light bulb comes on and it dawns on me that I'm right. Hey, I have to tell myself that I'm right because I never get to hear it from my wife...I love you, darling! I can't do everything and because of that, I must rely on God. I need Him to do what I can't, as long as it is according to His will.

The God that I serve is an unlimited God who can, all at once, be everywhere, see everything, and know everything. I, on the other hand, am a limited being. I know only the things that I've learned, I can only be one place at a time, and I can never see everything at once. My life had a beginning and one day it will have an end. It is because I am finite, that I need an infinite God to help me through life. I am what Jesus called "poor in spirit" in Matthew 5:3. I'm poor in abundance of life, in wisdom of the universe, and in so many ways, I'm poor when I compare myself to the God of the universe.

Those who are "poor in spirit" are in need of things. They need material things, spiritual things, and eternal things. The list could go on forever. So, God makes provision for us, the poor in spirit. He says that when we seek Him and really strive to get to KNOW Him and have a relationship with Him, He will provide for our daily needs.

> *But seek first the kingdom of God and His righteousness, and all these things will be provided for you.*
> Matthew 6:33 (HCSB)

In the passages leading up to Matthew 6:33, Jesus is telling his disciples that God is our ultimate provider and if we seek Him and His righteousness, we don't have to worry. If God will provide sustenance for the things of nature, then He will always be there to provide for His children.

Sometimes being faithful that God will fulfill that promise is difficult. Seriously, it's painstaking to wait for God to provide when we can't see evidence of His provision. When my son was an infant, I remember realizing that we were out of diapers and money. We had given our tithes to the church, we had all of our bills paid and we had groceries, but we had no money. For the parents reading this, you know that not having diapers for a small child is not really something that you just "work around."

I was stressed and didn't know what my wife and I were going to do. That afternoon, after worrying all day, I went home, checked the mail, and found a rebate check for $25.00. I don't remember who sent us the rebate or even why they did, but I do remember that we could buy diapers with $25.00. When I opened that envelope and saw the check, I got a little misty-eyed. I immediately thanked God for His provision because the money that we received was just enough to buy what we needed until the next payday.

God has always been faithful to His promise, even though I have not always trusted in Him completely. My family has always been a two-car family. My wife uses one to travel the 200 mile commute to and from work each day. I use the other one to take the kids to and from school on my days off. My car was always what we lovingly call a "cash car." Basically, it means that it was something with four wheels that would go.

In early 2012, we decided that we would upgrade to something that would go and maybe have a decent radio. The theme song to *The Jeffersons* is coming to mind right about now. Then, we found out that, due to chronic ear infections, my daughter had to have tubes put in her ears and also have her adenoids removed. At the time we had a high deductable insurance plan. The great part about most high deductable plans is that once that deductable is met, the insurance company will pay 100% of health costs for the rest of the year. Unfortunately, it was only January and we had not saved enough money for the deductable yet. We had recently sold my car and were preparing to upgrade, but instead we used the money we received to meet the deductable. Having the money for the surgery was a blessing, but having only one car was rough.

Later in the year, we were able to save up enough money for me to buy another very used "cash car." It lasted for about six months until the transmission went out, but even though I was doubtful, God remained faithful. My wife's parents had two vehicles and her step-father worked offshore most of the year. So, he offered to let me use one of their vehicles until we could save enough money to pay cash for another one. Here God goes again, being faithful. Our daughter got her surgery, and we had reliable transportation. When we seek God, His provision will come. It may come in the form of money, or it may come in the form of a borrowed vehicle, but He will be faithful.

It is necessary for me to explain that I have not always been able to trust God and His faithfulness. I guess that is where my flesh fails. As a child of the King, I know that He has what's best in store for me. I often pray for God to make my will line up with His will because, what I want and what He wants aren't always in line with each other. Because I ask God to make my will become His will, I don't often notice the immediate results of His provision. I feel as though He has to deny me things that I want, so that He can grant me the things that I need.

When things begin to work out the way they have for me, it is easy to fall into the snare of being boastful. It's easy to feel like I have it all together and have superhuman abilities to overcome adversity, but it's then that I have to remind myself that I'm only succeeding because I have an infinite God who values the seemingly insignificant. It is the despised and unimportant that He calls to greatness. He doesn't call the qualified. He qualifies the called.

*God has chosen what is insignificant and despised in the world—what is viewed as nothing—to bring to nothing what is viewed as something, so that no one can boast in His presence. But it is from Him that you are in Christ Jesus, who became God-given wisdom for us—our righteousness, sanctification, and redemption, in order that, as it is written: The one who boasts must boast in the Lord.*
1 Corinthians 1:28-31 (HCSB)

God can do much with little. When I was growing up, I always struggled with my weight and physical fitness. I was not morbidly obese, but I was definitely chubby. This was evident by the "husky" jeans that my mom had to buy for me when I was younger. I was always teased and called names because of my weight. One of the most "memorable" was Fat Matt. I can chuckle at it today, but back then, it really hurt. I wasn't sure that I would ever be able to amount to much.

Well, Jeremiah writes, "For I know the plans I have for you"—this is the Lord's declaration—"plans for your welfare, not for disaster, to give you a future and a hope. Jeremiah 29:11 (HCSB) God knew exactly what he was doing with this chubby little boy. He knew that I would eventually become a police officer because that is the calling I believe He placed upon my life. When I look back at the struggles of getting into the police academy (I failed the physical fitness portion of the entrance exam on my first try) I realize that God was setting me up, not for failure, but for success. At the time that I was attempting to go to the police academy, I was assigned to the Communications Division as a Dispatcher, but I really wanted to be on Patrol. When I failed to make it to the police academy, I felt as if I was missing out on so many opportunities. The longer that it took me to get to and through the academy, meant that it took me that much longer before I could transfer to the streets.

I was determined to persevere; I continued to train harder to perform better on the physical fitness portion of the entrance exam. After getting into the academy, I continued to struggle with the physical fitness portion. I remember having evaluations where I barely completed the required number of pushups. I eventually completed all of the requirements for the PT exam. The rest of the academy was not a struggle; I did well with the driving and firearms, and passed the Louisiana P.O.S.T. (Peace Officer's Standards and Training) exam with no problems.

After graduating from the academy in April of 2004, I didn't have to wait long until I got the phone call that I had been waiting for. I was being transferred to the Patrol Division. I completed my FTO training without any problems. I had good reviews and evaluations from all of my training officers.

After completing the FTO training, I was placed on a shift, and in typical rookie fashion, I was ready to arrest everyone. I was very "gung-ho" and there was no stopping me. I felt like a pit bull having to constantly be reigned in by my supervisors. I loved chasing dopers and the criminal element. If I wasn't working a complaint, I was making traffic stops.

There were times when my eagerness got me into trouble with my superiors. I was told to be a little more reactive, which was something that I didn't know how to do. In fact, after many years on the job, I still struggle with having to let the younger guys do all of the work. After being on patrol for a while and getting into trouble for being "too proactive," I decided that I wanted to transfer to the Special Crimes Apprehension Team (S.C.A.T.), which did, on a daily basis, what I wanted to do. Their job duties consisted of making traffic stops and conducting investigations to uncover crimes relating to street level narcotics and burglaries.

The problem with the situation was that I could want to transfer all day long, but there were no openings and it appeared that there would be no openings for a while. With no openings for a while, and the looming possibility of having to move out of town for my wife to finish school, I felt a sense of urgency and despair. I felt as though my time was running out and I would miss out on doing what I loved to do. Although I was not a Christian at the time, God knew what was in my future. I would not have to move out of town for my wife to finish school. I will tell you all about that little adventure in a later chapter. It was another one of those times when I struggled with believing God would be faithful to His promise and then actually waiting for that promise to come.

Getting back to the story at hand, after a couple of years of struggles with the supervisor that I tended to collide with about being proactive, he got transferred to be the supervisor over S.C.A.T. All I could think was, "Well great. I won't be making it over there any time soon." It's funny how God makes things happen because I got a call from him one night, the supervisor, not God, and he asked me if I wanted to be a part of the specialized unit. My initial reaction was one that I have heard from suspects before when I asked them a question: "Who, me?" After the initial shock of being asked, I gladly accepted my new position.

After a year and a half of hard work, God would bless me with my first promotion to Corporal in 2008 when I was 27 years old and then with my second promotion to Sergeant in 2010, which was just two months shy of my 29th birthday. My department is not, by any means, small and promotions don't come around too often and being promoted to a Sergeant at the age of 28 really doesn't happen very often. I was rising in the ranks faster than I expected, and I believe God made it happen. During this time, I would be able to partner with some really good deputies, who would help me hone my abilities and foster my God-given talents. So, as a result, what I saw as God being lax and "asleep at the wheel," was really Him preparing me to receive His blessings.

When I graduated from the academy, I was told by veteran officers that family should always come first. Although this is a well-meaning reminder, it left me focused on my purpose and not on God's purpose for my life. Instead, I must remember God should be my first priority and then my family. My first duty is to acknowledge that He is the provider of goodness and mercy in my life both personally and professionally, and as a result, I need to give Him all the glory.

Looking back at 1 Corinthians 1:29, Paul writes that no one should boast in His presence, which means that I have no right to glorify myself in front of God, because every good thing that I have attained in my life came from Him. This is confirmed in James 1:17 (HCSB), Every generous act and every perfect gift is from above, coming down from the Father of lights; with Him there is no variation or shadow cast by turning. The raises and promotions that were received based on my "outstanding abilities" are not because I am so great and wonderful, but because God is. After all, God gave me those abilities. Verse 30 says that as Christians, we are sanctified and redeemed in Christ Jesus. Through Jesus, I am able to enter into the presence of the Father and give Him the glory that is rightfully His. God created me and made a way for me to spend eternity in Heaven so that I can forever bask in His glory. How awesome is that? God made me nothing, so that I could fully acknowledge His glory.

Performing my duties as a police officer is one way I serve God, so my actions and character should exalt God and exemplify His love for all people. I must remember that I am not better than the lost people that I encounter or arrest. In fact, Paul says I'm insignificant. However, as a Christian, I am better off than those who are lost because I have been promised salvation, given by God through the death of his son, Jesus Christ.

*"Do nothing out of rivalry or conceit, but in humility consider others as more important than yourselves."*
Philippians 2:3 (HCSB)

When I put on my badge and gun and begin my shift, I strive to honor God, rather than to please people. If I put my focus on honoring and pleasing Him, I will always succeed. My job is about God, and not about me. This is especially hard to remember when I start to feel worn and burned out. Policing is a thankless job, and I have become accustomed to the idea that I'm more likely to receive complaints than commendations from the public. I can't count how many times I've heard, "Why don't you go catch some real criminals?"

I can remember one afternoon I was working a little overtime trying to make some extra money. I was doing traffic enforcement and I pulled a man over for running a stop sign. I wrote him a ticket and as I was explaining it to him and telling him how to contact the Traffic Bureau of the District Attorney's office, he got mad and told me that I should be out there catching people who are doing bad things instead of messing with him. At that time in my career, I was assigned to S.C.A.T., and as it just so happened that the night before, we had taken down three separate meth labs and put a whole lot of people in jail. After I told him about the previous night's events, the look on his face was priceless. It quickly shut down his "why are you picking on me" attitude.

This may not have been the most God-honoring way of handling the situation. Maybe I should have just ignored the man and went on my way, but to me it seemed important to let the man know that just because I wasn't dealing with a "serious criminal" at that moment it didn't mean that I don't ever deal with them. I suppose that it didn't occur to him that there have been many traffic fatalities because someone ran a stop sign or because they were speeding or because they were distracted by a text message. To me, the definition of "serious criminal" extends beyond drugs, rape and murder. Am I comparing a traffic violation with murder? No. Every crime has its own level of seriousness, but if I aggressively pursue smaller offenses, I might be able to prevent more serious crimes.

The general public has no idea what I do as a police officer from day to day. They have no insight into what a "day in the life" is really like, so they respond from their temporary frustration about their situation. It is my duty to remember that they are only seeing a small segment of what I'm doing. They can't possibly fully appreciate the work I'm doing...but God can. I can't lose sight of God when I work with the public, because I am not seeking their praise, I am seeking His. I'm seeking Him first. When I get worn out and burned out, I have to rely on God to carry me through.

*"God is our refuge and strength, a helper who is always found in times of trouble. "*

Psalm 46:1 (HCSB)

The Lord God is truly my refuge and strength. There have been times when I have called upon the Lord to help me through some difficult incidents. When the dispatcher comes over the radio with a call of, "All available units, be enroute to a disturbance-in-progress; the suspect is armed with a gun," I know two things: I need to get there quickly and I need to neutralize the situation safely. This is a great time to call upon the Lord for refuge. While enroute to the call, I often pray: "Lord, please keep everyone safe, including the bad guys, so that we may return home to love and care for our families. In Jesus' name I pray. Amen." It is not a lengthy or wordy prayer, but it certainly is sufficient to let the Lord know that I need Him.

I can remember calling on the Lord to keep my coworkers and me safe one afternoon during a vehicle pursuit that went into a neighboring parish. Yes, I said parish, not county; think back to geography class when you learned that Louisiana is the only state with parishes. The suspect fled from the scene of a traffic stop and the speeds reached the 120-130 MPH range. Was I nervous? You better believe it. But, after a quick prayer to God asking for our safety, I felt a sense of peace and calm come over me. I knew that the Holy Spirit was with us and that there would be a positive outcome. The pursuit ended in the driveway of the suspect's house, and he was taken into custody without any further incident.

People can't possibly know the dangers I face each day. There are often times when I'm responding to a "hot call," where I'll be driving at dangerous speeds between unpredictable drivers or when I'm about to enter a door, not sure of what's on the other side. There are times when I'm afraid and need to be comforted. I need to calm down before I face the adversary. I need God to provide me refuge and calm so that I can do my job. When I call on Him, He answers. He fills me with peace, and I'm able to do my job rather than standing there, paralyzed with fear.

God is my provider, the reason for my successes. I am blessed by God when I surrender to Him and recognize the poverty of my spirit. I seek God and His righteousness, and He responds with all of the things I need. He provides for my material needs, spiritual needs, and my eternal needs. He does not allow me to be boastful. Instead, He expects humility from me and if I lose sight of Him, He will remind me of my insignificance. It's only by God that I do my job well, and when I do my job well, I honor Him.

*"I command the married—not I, but the Lord—a wife is not to leave her husband. But if she does leave, she must remain unmarried or be reconciled to her husband—and a husband is not to leave his wife."*
1 Corinthians 7:10-11 (HCSB)

# THEY'RE ALL YOURS

## *CHAPTER 2*

Okay, so I need to give you a disclaimer here. The premise of this book is to apply the Beatitudes to policing, but many of the experiences in this chapter will extend beyond that. Most of the stories in this chapter are about circumstances in my personal life, but I feel that having a stable personal life can lead to having a stable professional life. I just can't ignore these things because they are a big part of my journey, and in many ways if I am applying the Beatitudes to my life, then I am striving to be as Christ-like as possible. So, I'm going to discuss priorities as God sees them. These priorities are not directly addressed in the Beatitudes, but God does instruct us in other places of the Bible, like the Old Testament, in terms of how we should organize our priorities. The first priority should be God and putting Him above all else, but after that comes family.

*"Therefore a man will leave his father and his mother, and will join with his wife, and they will be one flesh."*
Genesis 2:24 (WEB)

When I return home at the end of my shift, all I want to do is relax and unwind, but my wife and family need my attention. Luckily for me, my wife is a Psychologist who does work with inmates and police officers. Her work helps her understand that I need a little space before I am able to really get involved with them. Many officers don't have this luxury because their spouses don't understand the demands of the job and expect them to come home and immediately transition from police duties into family duties.

My wife notices my moods and wants to know about my day, especially if she suspects that "something happened." On the days when something tragic happens at work, my wife tries to understand my mood change by relating it to one of her bad days at work. Unfortunately, without actually experiencing it firsthand, she can't possibly know the kind of tragedy I may have encountered. I try hard to distance myself from the feelings that I have in those moments so that I can focus on my family, but when I don't want to talk about it she sometimes feels like I'm distancing myself from her. It's important for me to help her understand my coping process by telling her that initially I need a little space, but that I'll be happy to talk to her when I feel ready.

*"Wives, be submissive to your husbands, as is fitting in the Lord. Husbands, love your wives and don't be bitter toward them. "*
Colossians 3:18-19 (HCSB)

There have been times when I came home from a stressful shift and the only thing I wanted to do was sit on the couch and vegetate in front of the television, but as soon as I came through the door, the kids wanted me to play with them and my wife wanted me to help her with whatever she was doing. On days like that, I had to explain to my family that I needed time to gather myself and hang up the work day's problems and stresses in the closet. When I didn't have enough transition time between work and family, I caught myself being grumpy with my family and began to see them as more of an annoyance than a pleasure, especially when they got in the way of my rest and relaxation. However, when I told my family that I needed some space, I was able to unwind and then show them the love and attention they needed.

Communication with my family about my needs has been crucial. Sometimes, I didn't really want to talk to my family about what I was feeling or tell them my needs, but shutting them out never worked out real well. Shutting them out made them feel unimportant, and I felt annoyed. Family is my way of separating from the stresses of the job. They are my source of support. As an officer, I have a lot of enemies and few friends, so I can't isolate myself from the few supportive people I do have.

Managing to meet all of our needs has been tricky, but we've found a solution that seems to work for us. At the end of the day, my wife needs me to spend time with her, our children need my attention, and I need to relax. So, I sit outside in my patio chair "talking" to my wife (that really means listening while she talks) while we watch the kids play in the tree house. Everyone's needs are met. It is usually a win, win, win situation. I get to enjoy the fresh air and breezes of the outdoors, which I find relaxing. My wife gets the quality time that she needs from me while I listen to her tell me about her day (I am a GREAT listener). The kids enjoy showing me the cool tricks that they have learned to do on the swings and slide. I can listen to my wife, praise my children, and watch them play, without leaving the comfort of my patio chair, until I feel rested enough to become physically and emotionally active with them.

After sitting in a police car all day, physical activity helps me reduce my stress. This is especially true for me since I have struggled with my weight for most of my life. So, I have to remind myself not to get stuck sitting in that patio chair indefinitely. After I've had some time to recover, I might try playing catch with the kids or playfully wrestling with them. Being active with my kids helps me to connect with them and to distance myself from work. I look for creative ways to relieve stress while being able to spend time with my family.

My son likes to pretend that he is a teacher, and he will mimic the gym coach at his school. Recently, my son had my wife and me outside in the yard doing "P.E. class" with him as the "coach." Another time, he had us "running track" around the trees in the backyard. The possibilities are endless. This achieved so many goals. I interacted with my son and got in some exercise at the same time. It was also funny seeing my "little man" pretending to be the coach.

*"A man with many friends may be harmed, but there is a friend who stays closer than a brother. "*
Proverbs 18:24 (HCSB)

Over the years, I've begun to lose touch with my non-police friends. I was warned that this might happen when I graduated from the academy, but I doubted that it was true for me because those people were important to me. They were best friends in high school; they walked beside me during my wedding. I thought to myself, "Of course I wouldn't forget them," but I did.

In some cases, working graveyards caused distance in my friendships, and in others, my oath to serve and protect was directly responsible for the end of a friendship. As a police officer, some of the things that I have seen (e.g. death and destruction) and done (e.g. giving CPR to a lifeless child) can only be understood by other cops; therefore, I have been drawn to other officers who can understand and relate to my experiences. It's hard for me to enjoy hanging out with people who can't relate to my profession. Unfortunately for me, my wife's profession is similar. So, over the years we found ourselves hanging out with cops and cynical therapists. What an exciting and happy bunch we were!

Our limited circle of friends was not always a good thing for me. They were just as pessimistic as I was, and when we were together we could, at times; see people as problems rather than humans. The therapists broke this up a little, but not very much despite their efforts. Cops don't usually get called to people's houses during happy times. No one calls me because they want me to share birthday cake or open Christmas presents with them. I get called to clean up messes. So, I began to forget that good people exist and to think that the only "good" people left in the world were other cops.

As time progressed, I noticed that my co-workers and I needed to be drinking any time we were together. It was almost like we couldn't have a good time without drinking. We faced so many ugly things and had so little opportunity to relax, that we seemed to need to be numb to have fun. We looked to alcohol to numb our pain and help us relax, because we'd forgotten how we were before we were bound by the badge. It would usually start out as "just a beer," which turned into three, which progressed to a mixed drink, which led to more and more to the point of excess.

I drank because I didn't know how to relax or be a part of a group without it. It was what police officers did. Drinking never really helped though. I had moments of fun, but mostly I woke up feeling bad the next morning and still didn't know how to deal with the pain of my experiences or how to relate to my family the way I needed to.

*"Therefore encourage one another and build each other up as you are already doing. "*
1 Thessalonians 5:11 (HCSB)

After several years of policing, I was drained with constantly being surrounded by and consumed with law enforcement. At that time in my life, I was also spiritually unfulfilled. My wife kept telling me that she wanted to "get into church" and I didn't want to hear it, but I gave in and told her that we could try some churches. I clarified that I wanted to go to a church that clearly outlined their mission and the activities that were available to us as a young, married couple with a baby.

My wife had a friend (a fellow psychologist, as it would turn out) who kept inviting us to come to church with her. So, I finally agreed to go. To my surprise, after the opening prayers and worship music, the lead pastor stood in front of the congregation and said that he was going to do something a little different that morning: He was going to state the mission of the church and tell everyone about the "care groups" that were available. Isn't it amazing how God knows our stipulations and is prepared to answer them?

By this time in the service, my wife and I were just staring at each other with amazement. We almost, in unison, said that we were there to stay. We've been members at the church for a little more than six years now. Throughout those years, we've developed many relationships and gained many new friends who are not in law enforcement. I truly believe that God led my wife and me to our church and put us in the pew on that particular morning. I thank God that He led us to a great church where we have many friends, where we are able to fellowship in the Lord, and where we are able to receive the fulfilling Word of God.

The friends we made at church have supported us through difficult times and celebrated with us when things were going well. They aren't cynical and jaded. Instead, they are hopeful and optimistic. Hanging out with them helps me to remember that there are people in the world who are not criminals. Our friends also know how to have a good time, without drinking. Through their fellowship, they've taught me how to relax and be part of a group. Having these friends to balance out my police friends helps me to see the world more positively and to be less distrustful.

*But if anyone does not provide for his own, that is his own household, he has denied the faith and is worse than an unbeliever.*
1Timothy 5:8 (HCSB)

Wow! Those are really strong words. If you're at all like me, you read those words and patted yourself on the back for really providing for your family, but I want to challenge that thought for a minute. You may, in fact, make enough money to provide for your family, but how much of YOU are you giving your family? Earlier, I talked about finding creative ways of being present with my family after work. The thing my family needs above anything else is my presence and guidance, but how can I provide those things if I'm never home?

Several years ago, between my regular shift and overtime, I worked over 100 hours in a week. I was exhausted! My paycheck was very nice and I was providing for my family's financial needs, but what I wasn't doing was providing for their emotional needs. I was grumpy most of the time and wanted to be left alone because I was tired. I had absolutely no energy to play with my son or interact with my wife. This left my wife working her daily job, providing for all of our son's needs, and doing the household chores. She was exhausted and needed my support, attention, and presence in her life.

This situation was not unusual for us. I was never around because I was always working or sleeping. I can remember coming home at 2 A.M. and heading back to work four hours later at 6 A.M. for another 18 hour day. I missed several milestones of my son's life, and I will never regain that time. Leaving so little time for my family left me and my wife feeling unfulfilled, empty, and distant. My wife didn't have the energy to meet my needs, and I was neglecting hers. Over time, our marriage became a strain, and I started looking elsewhere for satisfaction and fulfillment.

*"You have heard that it was said, Do not commit adultery. But I tell you, everyone who looks at a woman to lust for her has already committed adultery with her in his heart."*
Matthew 5:27 (HCSB)

I have been faced with many temptations during my time in policing. The one temptation that I struggled with the most was sexual temptation. I never physically cheated on my wife, but working long hours and having an exhausted wife left little time for us to nurture our romantic and sexual relationship. So, I looked to pornography. I always thought it was a harmless way to have my needs met, without "cheating" on my wife. It was harmless, right? Well, pornography is absolutely not harmless. I began looking occasionally as a "quick fix" and an easy way to fall asleep, but over time I needed more and more until I eventually became addicted.

I don't remember exactly how old I was when I first saw pornography, but I know I was young. I remember finding magazines with nude pictures in them and later pornographic videos. That was the start of a 20+ year addiction to pornography. I continued to view pornography after I married my wife. I never thought that I was hurting anyone, and my wife knew that I indulged in such activity, but she seemed not to care, as long as I wasn't "bothering" her. What I didn't know is that when I watched pornography, she was hurt. She felt as though I was comparing her to the women on the computer and as though I wanted her to become someone she wasn't comfortable being.

She told me later how much it hurt her emotionally for me to watch pornography. She began to feel that there was no need for her to meet my needs, because she would never be able to satisfy me the way the videos could. She became more and more distant and less and less emotionally available to me. I may not have had sex with other women, but she knew of my fantasies and doubted her own attractiveness and my desire for her. In some ways, she emotionally checked out of our marriage. I didn't realize it, but my addiction was definitely causing harm.

The more she emotionally "checked out," the more I felt that I "needed" the pornography. She didn't want sex, but I certainly did. We were both tired and I could save her the trouble by watching porn until the hard financial times passed and I was able to work less. I was still attracted to her, but we were never together and pornography was a quick and easy solution to my sexual frustrations. I still believed I wasn't hurting anyone.

*"No temptation has taken you except what is common to man. God is faithful, who will not allow you to be tempted above what you are able, but will with the temptation also make the way of escape, that you may be able to endure it."*
1 Corinthians 10:13 (WEB)

After we started going to church, I eventually gave my life to Christ and started reading my Bible. Over time, I began to feel conviction about viewing pornography, but I struggled to stop until I realized that I was never going to grow spiritually while using pornography. It was then that I asked God and my wife to help me overcome my addiction. I prayed to God often, telling Him my honest feelings and thoughts. My wife and I also had open discussions about my addiction. She was understanding, forgiving, and willing to help me. She became my accountability partner and my prayer partner. My testimony is that by the healing power of Jesus Christ, I was able to overcome my addiction and no longer view pornography.

As we worked together to strengthen our marriage and eliminate pornography, we learned that we needed help learning how to show our love for each other. Don't get me wrong here, I was (and still very much am) totally in love with my wife, but I didn't know how to show her that I loved her. As a long time student my wife learns by reading, so off to the bookstore we went. We found a book by Dr. Gary Chapman called *The Five Love Languages* which helped us tremendously. Dr. Chapman pointed out that everyone shows their love differently, and that everyone expects to receive love differently. Each night, we sat in our bed and read the book out loud to each other and then discussed the points that resonated with us. We continued this until the book was finished. Taking this approach helped us communicate better. We still check in with one another about our "love tanks."

Communication began there, but it didn't stop there. We have learned to talk openly with one another about our feelings and the challenges that we face. It's our goal to talk with one another about everything, before little problems become insurmountable ones. We have learned to talk openly about our feelings even when what we're feeling may be hurtful. Honesty helps us to avoid feeling resentful and bitter toward one another. Instead, we say what we feel and try to work out a plan for making things better. We actively work to keep the love in our marriage.

Although the importance of family is not directly mentioned in the Sermon on the Mount, it is mentioned in the Bible. I believe that after putting God first, it's important to focus on the family. If you're married, I would encourage you to be willing to share the struggles of policing with your spouse. Even if they are not a professional counselor, like mine is, your spouse can be your supporter. They can give you a listening ear when you want to vent frustrations or need to release some emotions you are feeling after "something happened" at work. If you have a family, please be an involved parent with your kids. Love on them, interact with them and engage them. Those early milestones are treasures that can never be replaced. I missed a few by working too much. I don't plan on missing out on any more because I have realized that time passes too quickly and before I know it, my children will be grown. If you find yourself being caught up by working too many hours and missing out on those milestones, you can change things because today is a new day. Get involved and be active with your kids, they will love it!

Surround yourself with positive and encouraging people. Being a police officer means being surrounded by the negative and discouraging influences of the world. A good group of friends that you can spend time with away from work will be very beneficial to your health by allowing you to leave the stresses of work where they belong, at work. Remember that when physical temptations arise, please resist them. If your spouse is not providing for your physical needs, don't turn to other means of fulfillment. It will only get in the way of your relationship. Talk with your spouse about your needs and seek to have open communication with them.

When I found Jesus Christ, I found the fulfillment I had been looking for in alcohol and pornography. The joy and peace that I had been searching for was there all along, I just wasn't looking in the right place. As police officers, we find ourselves in situations where we may have to rescue someone. I didn't, however, realize that I would be the one that needed rescuing. Jesus rescued me and saved me from habits that were leading me to destruction. If you find yourself in personal or professional circumstances that seem too overwhelming or unbearable, He can rescue you too!

*"May integrity and what is right watch over me, for I wait for You."*
Psalm 25:21 (HCSB)

# EVEN WHEN

## NO ONE IS LOOKING
### CHAPTER 3

*"Blessed are the pure in heart, for they shall see God."*
Matthew 5:8 (WEB)

What does being pure in heart have to do with being a police officer? Well, it has to do with integrity. Since police officers are in a position of significant power, it's crucial to do this job with integrity. When I worked on S.C.A.T., my job was to seek out the criminal element, mostly in the form of drug dealers/users and burglars. When I dealt with illegal narcotics, I was very careful to maintain the highest level of integrity when dealing with the evidence.

One night I stopped a guy after he left one of the well-known crack houses in our area. While talking to him, I got one of those "feelings" that I usually got when I believed someone to be in possession of illegal drugs. I searched his truck and all of his pockets. I found in his pants pocket a crumpled dollar bill. In my past experiences "crumpled" equaled "concealed". I carefully opened the bill and found a very small piece of crack. After I field tested it to determine that it was crack, there was just enough to log into evidence. My thought process was: "After taking this small piece of crack and testing it, there is barely enough to log into evidence, and after the crime lab tests it, will there be any left to present as evidence at trial?"

I had made another arrest for possession of crack cocaine earlier in the evening, and that evidence was still locked in my trunk. I could have easily taken a small piece of evidence from that case and put it into the evidence associated with the current investigation. It is likely that no one would have ever known, but the problem was that I would have known and more importantly God would have known. And if I would've tampered with the evidence and someone found out about it, my integrity and reputation for not only future cases, but past cases as well, would have been called into question.

I made the arrest based on the little evidence that was left. I remember getting a crime lab report that confirmed that the evidence submitted was in fact crack cocaine, but I don't remember if the district attorney's office prosecuted the case. At least I did my job with the utmost integrity.

When dealing with drug dealers, I quite often seized money that I believed to be proceeds from drug sales. I stopped a guy on the interstate one afternoon and I found two ounces of high grade marijuana, a loaded firearm, and a large amount of cash. I took the dope and gun as evidence and seized the money for forfeiture. Before I counted it, I asked the guy how much money he had. He told me that it was about $7,000 and looking at the wad of cash, I believed that he would be accurate. After booking the guy into jail, I took the money back to my office to get an accurate count. After counting the money, I reached a total of $12,379.00. I had to count it again to make sure that I didn't count some of it twice.

I was put into the position of having about $5,000 more than what the bad guy thought that he had. I could have easily not turned in the difference and reported the $7,000 that the man thought that he had. Again, no one would have known, but had I done that and someone found out about it, my integrity and reputation would have been questioned, and I likely would have found myself sitting in jail as well.

Even when no one is watching, or those times when we think that no one is watching, honor and integrity are of the upmost importance. It's not my job to use my position for my own selfish motive or illegal gain, but to do the good which God has called me to do.

*"...for he is a servant of God to you for good. But if you do that which is evil, be afraid, for he doesn't bear the sword in vain; for he is a servant of God, an avenger for wrath to him who does evil."*

Romans 13:4 (WEB)

When I put on my uniform each day, I leave my house and begin my work as a servant, called by God "for good," to administer justice, or at least to begin the process of administering justice. I am an "avenger for wrath." That whole "avenger for wrath" thing makes me sound like a super-hero who goes out saving the world from evil and fighting for truth and justice. Well, being a cop is kind of like being a super-hero. I do fight evil, and I do seek truth and justice. An "avenger" is someone who inflicts punishment in return for an injury or offense[3]. So, when people do bad things, it is my job to initiate punishment on them by placing them under arrest and starting the process of justice. "Wrath" is retributory punishment for a crime[4.] So, when God called me to law enforcement, He chose me to be someone who initiates the punishment of a wrongdoer for a crime.

When I read Romans 13:4, it was interesting to me that God first stated that I am a servant of God, to you...for good. He talked about how I am to do "good," before He talked about punishment. For me, that means that it is my responsibility to do my job in a God honoring way. I am not to be abusive in my actions because I am called "for good."

If I am one of God's ministers of justice, I'm fighting evil on His behalf and with His authority. It is true that God gave each of us the ability to freely choose our actions, but Satan knows how to exploit our weaknesses and tempt us with evil. So, when people (either good or bad) do bad things, yes, I am exacting punishment on them, but it is important for me to remember that I am really fighting Satan, who has exploited them and is seeking to destroy them. I am not fighting against the person; I am, with the help and authority of God, fighting the evil that afflicts them.

*"We know that all things work together for the good of those who love God: those who are called according to His purpose."*

Romans 8:28 (HCSB)

39

What stands out to me in Romans 8:28 is that ALL things work together for those who love God and to those who are CALLED according to His purpose. It seems to me that in Romans, I am being taught to trust that ultimately, God plans for me to prosper in some way, even when I can't imagine how. Everything that happens to me, good or bad, is meant to help me become the person God has planned. I don't think this verse is saying that God is going to always give me what I want or make my life easy. Instead, I think God is saying that I need to trust that everything that happens in my life has a purpose. Then, I think He is saying that He has called me to live out that purpose. He directs me to live out His divine will for my life.

Confirmation of God's goodness can be found in Psalms 84:11-12, HCSB which says, "For the Lord God is a sun and shield; The Lord gives grace and glory; He does not withhold the good from those who live with integrity. Happy is the person who trusts in You, Lord of Hosts." When I end my shift, if I can stand with my head held high, and know that I performed my duties in a manner that would be pleasing and honorable to God, He will give me His grace and glory. Since God is always true to His word, I can trust Him to provide grace, glory, and blessings. Being pure in heart is about integrity, but it is also about helping others and not being selfish.

*"Defend the weak, the poor, and the fatherless. Maintain the rights of the poor and oppressed. Rescue the weak and needy. Deliver them out of the hand of the wicked."*
Psalm 82:3-4 (WEB)

Not only as a police officer, but as God's minister of justice, I have the duty to defend the needy and fatherless (orphans). Here come the thoughts of being a super-hero again. When I read that I am to defend the "fatherless," I take that to mean not only people who don't know their biological fathers, but also those who don't know their Heavenly Father. I am to free the poor and needy from the hand of the wicked.

Freeing people from the hand of the wicked might mean removing a child from an abusive home, helping a person involved in a domestic violence situation, or assisting someone with finding rehabilitation for a drug or alcohol addiction. At times, people need to be freed from someone else, but at other times, they need to be delivered from themselves. Being pure in heart has to do with integrity and the motives behind actions. It is the opposite of selfishness or illegal gain. It is serving God in a way that is honoring to Him and doing the good that is required of me as His servant. By striving to be pure in heart, I can truly see God.

> *"Even though I walk through the valley of the shadow of death, I will fear no evil, for you are with me. Your rod and your staff, they comfort me."*
>
> Psalm 23:4 (WEB)

# WHEN THE END

---

## IS JUST THE BEGINNING        CHAPTER 4

> *"Blessed are those who mourn, for they shall be comforted."*
>
> Matthew 5:4 (WEB)

During the evening hours on March 4, 2010, I was standing in the patrol briefing room of my department. I was there because my unit had broken down, and I was trying to get another one so that I could finish working my extra duty detail. That's when it happened; the moment that would impact so many lives. There is no greater disheartening feeling than hearing the following words come over the radio: "Shots fired! Officer down!" I grabbed the keys to a random police car that was on the back lot, and I raced out of the office to provide assistance. There was a mixture of emotions that came over me while I was driving to the scene. I was angry at the drivers who were in the way and wouldn't yield to my lights and siren. I was worried about not knowing what was happening at the scene. I remember that I prayed to God for Him to allow everyone to be safe and unharmed.

When I arrived on the scene, I remember being one of the first responding units. I could see three deputies kneeling around another deputy who was laying on the ground. They were near the front of a car that was parked in the driveway of the residence, and as I ran around the front quarter panel, I could see what happened: Corporal J.R. Searcy had been shot. A quick glance across the front yard let me know that the suspect was also shot and it was apparent that he was deceased.

I knew that I would be in the way if I tried to help J.R., but I needed to do something. I took on the task of gathering witnesses – which were family members of the suspect – and escorting them from the crime scene. I made sure to carefully document each person who was inside of the crime scene area at the time of the shooting, and I made sure to document who entered and exited after the crime scene tape went up. This was my way of "helping" and it also allowed me to stay busy.

A plethora of police officers would eventually arrive on the scene. Not only were there deputies from the Sheriff's Office, but officers from surrounding municipalities and troopers from the Louisiana State Police showed up as well. After J.R. was taken to the hospital by ambulance, the crowd thinned as most of them went to the hospital to support each other and J.R.'s family.

The hardest part of the next several hours would be the not knowing. Not knowing if J.R. would survive. Not knowing if he did survive, to what extent he would recover. The not knowing was burdensome. I stayed on the scene until about 3 o'clock the next morning while the crime scene technicians documented every piece of evidence. When I left the scene that night, I said a prayer of thanksgiving. I was thankful that God protected the responding officers, me included, as we rushed to the scene. Although the earlier events were tragic, I was thankful that no one else was hurt.

Over the course of the next few days, I learned that J.R. would not survive the shooting. He was on life support at one of the local hospitals while doctors were waiting to harvest his organs. I reflect, now, on the fact that in losing his life, J.R. was able to give life to others. I remember standing guard at his bedside for a few hours while the final word from the organ harvest team was being awaited. I felt troubled because I was not there when the shooting happened. I felt as though somehow my presence could have made the difference between life and death. I suppose my feelings were a product of survivor's guilt; but in the months and years that would pass, I came to understand that my presence at the scene that day was not God's will.

J.R.'s funeral service was attended by hundreds of officers. The overwhelming part about the officers who were in attendance was the fact that many of them came from different states to support the deputies of our department and pay their respects to the Searcy family. The funeral procession

44

to the cemetery was longer than any I had seen or even heard of before; it stretched for miles.

My wife was with me at the graveside services. After the twenty-one gun salute, after the procession with the horse without a rider, and after the folding of the flag came the one thing that brought forth all of the emotion that I had been bottling up - hearing J.R.'s call sign, 0831, over the radio. The radio crackles, "164 to 0831." No response. The radio crackles again, "164 to 0831." Again, there was no response. For a third and final time I hear, "164 to 0831." With no response, the radio traffic is as follows: "164 to Headquarters." The dispatcher replied, "Go ahead, 164." The supervisor replies, "Log 0831, 10-7, 10-42." In plain language, this meant that J.R. was out of service at his residence. Burying my face into my wife's shoulder, I broke into tears. Not the tears that we repress while trying to be strong for others, but the weeping and crying of sadness that comes with loss. I was finally able to allow myself to mourn for the loss of a fellow officer.

The outpouring of support from the community was impressive. Throughout the astonishingly long funeral procession, citizens lined both sides of the route. They waved American flags, and held signs that showed their support to J.R.'s family and to the department. There were thousands of people standing in the heat to support a fallen public servant. It seemed like the entire city had shut down that day.

*"Jesus said to her, "I am the resurrection and the life. He who believes in me will still live, even if he dies. Whoever lives and believes in me will never die. Do you believe this?"*
John 11:25-26 (WEB)

While writing and doing research for this book, I got a copy of the video of J.R.'s funeral services. Chaplain Scott Thompson spoke on this very verse. It is interesting to mention that I did not remember Scott speaking on John 11:25-26 until I watched the video, which was a little over three years after the service. I had selected this verse for this chapter many months prior to reviewing the video and being reminded of the service.

Chaplain Thompson's message was one of assurance and hope. He gave us assurance in knowing that J.R. had given his life to Jesus Christ. He gave us assurance in knowing that J.R. understood that we have all sinned, and fall short of the glory of God (Romans 3:23, WEB), and because of that he had accepted Jesus as his Lord and Savior. He gave us hope in knowing that because scripture tells us, "For everyone who calls on the name of the Lord will be saved." (Romans 10:13, HCSB); we could rest easy knowing that J.R. was in Heaven with Jesus.

*"Then we who are still alive will be caught up together with them in the clouds to meet the Lord in the air and so we will always be with the Lord. Therefore encourage one another with these words."*
1 Thessalonians 4:17-18 (HCSB)

All too often, as police officers, we lose brothers and sisters in the line of duty. We are then left with the question: "Did they go to heaven?" I once told my wife that when I die, I didn't want people to say that I went to heaven because it would help them with the grieving process, but I wanted people to be sure that I went to heaven because they knew, without a doubt, that I belonged to Jesus Christ! I want my life to be a reflection of my Heavenly Father.

We will discuss in a later chapter, the importance of evangelizing. We MUST reach the lost! We are given the commission by Jesus to do so. Just as we don't want to die and go to hell, we shouldn't want others to die and go to hell either.

*"He will wipe away from them every tear from their eyes. Death will be no more; neither will there be mourning, nor crying, nor pain, any more. The first things have passed away."*
Revelation 21:4 (WEB)

Death is the ultimate freedom for Christians. It is not the end, but the joyous beginning. It marks the beginning of our relationship with God in the everlasting. It is the time when we are free from crying tears of sadness, when we are free from mourning, and when we are free from mental, physical, and emotional pain. We will be able to rejoice in His presence and give Him all of the honor, glory, and praise that are rightfully His. Even when tragedy strikes, I can know that there is comfort because with Jesus Christ, the end is just the beginning!

*He leads the humble in what is
right and teaches them His way.*
Psalm 25:9

*"One who is slow to anger is better than the mighty; one who rules his spirit, than he who takes a city."*
Proverbs 16:32 (WEB)

# WHO IS

## IN CONTROL HERE?                    CHAPTER 5

*"Blessed are the meek: for they shall inherit the earth."*
Matthew 5:5 (KJV)

As a police officer, I am supposed to be meek and gentle until the time comes when I don't need to be. Meekness is the same as weakness, right? Well, that statement would be wrong. "Biblical meekness is not weakness but rather refers to exercising God's strength under His control – i.e. demonstrating power without undue harshness[5]." It is important for me to understand where I get my strength, which is from God, and how to control it so that I don't abuse my power. I have no problem knowing and understanding that God gives me strength, but as a human being who falls short from time to time, I can forget how to control it. My actions may have temporary effects on people, but my words can last longer. I have to constantly remind myself to be controlled.

*"Therefore, God's chosen ones, holy and loved, put on heartfelt compassion, kindness, humility, gentleness, and patience,"*
Colossians 3:12 (HCSB)

Like me, you can probably relate to being in situations where you were on the verge of losing your temper with someone. Well, I have actually crossed that line and completely lost my temper with other people. I use the word crossed, but others might say leaped, jumped, or catapulted. I'm not referring to physically "beating someone down", but I have handed out several tongue lashings. It wasn't always with people on the streets that I lost my temper. I've "gone off" on my coworkers as well. How bone-headed could I have been? I've completely lost my cool with the very people who were going to be watching my back in dangerous situations. This can create a poor working relationship between me and other deputies, but as a supervisor, if I needlessly use harsh words it can cause those who work under me to lose respect for me and cause those above me to question my leadership abilities.

In the introduction, I told you that I would share stories of times when I failed to rise to the occasion of exemplifying Christ. Here is one of those times. Shortly after being promoted to Sergeant, I was in a period of finding my place between being a "working deputy" and a "supervisor," that's not to say that I didn't work as a supervisor. I was dissatisfied with the actions and behavior of some of my team members, so I called for a team meeting. As I was admonishing them for something that happened the previous night, I felt my blood pressure rise. It rose to the point of telling my guys that if they didn't like the way things were going to be done then there was the (expletive) door, pointing angrily toward the open door to our office.

I realized that this "meeting" was not going to be productive, so we all left without much being accomplished. I found out that my supervisor, who was present during the meeting, was not really happy with the way that I conducted myself. I also found out that the Major over the Patrol Division was really not happy with what I had done. After some time had passed and I was able to reflect upon my conduct, I realized that I was wrong. I was wrong, not necessarily for wanting my men to understand the command and control structure, but for the "undue harshness" that I used. I have been on the receiving end of several tongue lashings, some of them deserved and some of them not, but after getting "chewed out" I always felt horrible. It was so demeaning to have someone in authority, who I was supposed to look up to and respect, verbally tear me down. That is exactly what I did to my team members. Realizing that I was wrong, I had to swallow my pride and go to them and apologize for the way that I treated them. I received forgiveness from everyone, but it reminded me of driving nails into a wooden board. You can take them out, but there will always be a mark.

Colossians 3:12 tells me that as someone chosen by God I am to have kindness and patience. During one of my rookie years, before I became a Christian, I can remember having a bad day at work. This was one of the bad days where I didn't want to be around anyone and basically hated the world. One night while on patrol, I made a traffic stop for a minor violation. Let's stop right here for a moment. Was this a problem? You bet it was. If you are having a bad day and are angry about someone or something, don't make traffic stops until you have reconciled your issue. Well, just as my luck would have it, the guy I stopped was drunk and I ended up arresting him for DWI. The problem was that he was not one of those "happy drunks" – the ones who just love everybody when they are lit. He was quite the opposite and had a way of really pushing my buttons.

I finally had enough of him and I slammed my fist on the desk and told him to be quiet. Well, it was not as polite and "G-rated" as that, but you get the picture. This guy jumps up from his chair in the room where we were doing the breath test and he is ready to fight! Luckily my partner was there to calm us both down.

Looking back on the situation later, I was embarrassed. I acted very unprofessionally and again, although not a Christian at the time, I was not honoring God with my actions. I had no kindness. I had no patience. I allowed my attitude to interfere with my professionalism.

"*Rejoice in hope; be patient in affliction; be persistent in prayer.*"
Romans 12:12 (HCSB)

Not only am I supposed to be patient with people, but with the circumstances that affect my life. In the latter part of 2009, I was working as a Corporal on S.C.A.T. and this type of work required me to be on the night shift. At the same time, my wife had a night class in school, which was going to last for several months. The conflicting schedule was putting a strain on my home life. I did not get to see my wife very often, and my son was having trouble adjusting to the lack of structure.

I went to my supervisors and requested a transfer out of the unit and back onto Patrol, where I could work the day shift. This greatly helped my home life, and my son got a lot happier. While on patrol, though, I was struggling with my situation. I liked working on the specialized unit, and I was quickly becoming bored with answering barking dog and harassing phone call complaints on patrol. Those things seemed so menial to me. I wanted to be doing something that "mattered." I always got personal fulfillment out of solving thefts, burglaries, and robberies. I got so much joy out of recovering stolen property, especially guns, and being able to return it to the rightful owner. I decided that I wanted to transfer from Patrol to Investigations, so I put in a letter requesting the transfer, but it didn't happen. I was frustrated and didn't know what to do.

As 2009 turned into 2010, I was at a loss. Then in April, I got a phone call from the Patrol Commander. He called me into his office and wanted to know if I would consider going back to S.C.A.T. Since this meant having to go back to the night shift, I told him that I would have to check with my wife to see what her school schedule had in store for the future. The commander even sweetened the deal with a promotion to a supervisory position.

I immediately called my wife and told her of the news. I was super excited, but did not want to get my hopes up too high, because her school schedule might have prevented the transfer. She told me that she would be going to a normal schedule and would not have any more night classes.

God rewarded my patience with my situation and granted me the opportunity to go back to the specialized unit that I enjoyed; He blessed me with a promotion, which meant two things: I was able to move up in rank, and I got a raise in pay.

*"Be silent before the Lord and wait expectantly for Him; do not be agitated by one who prospers in his way, by the man who carries out evil plans. Refrain from anger and give up your rage; do not be agitated—it can only bring harm. For evildoers will be destroyed, but those who put their hope in the Lord will inherit the land."*
Psalm 37:7-9 (HCSB)

The profession of policing is one where I am constantly in contact with people who are unrighteous, whether it is the public or my coworkers, and I can occasionally make the mistake of envying them. Remember the guy I mentioned in chapter 3 about having the large amount of money? It was obvious to me that he was a drug dealer and that was his "job." At the time of this incident, I was struggling, financially, to make ends meet and get all of my family's bills paid. It was disheartening and frustrating to see someone who makes a living at illegal activity to be prosperous when I am struggling while working 50+ hours per week at a real job.

There was one day in particular that I was having a hard time with this. It seemed that everything was going right for the unrighteous, while everything in my world was falling apart. When I got home that evening, I was sitting in bed holding my Bible. I knew that I needed a Word from God, but I didn't even know where to begin looking. I closed my eyes and opened my Bible. The first passage that I saw was Proverbs 23:17, HCSB which said, "Don't let your heart envy sinners; instead, always fear the Lord." I immediately knew that God was speaking to me and that this verse was what I needed to help me through my struggle.

In the end, I have to remember that being meek doesn't mean that I am to be spineless and allow people to walk all over me, but to take the strength that God gives me and use it in a kind and gentle manner. When I find myself to be discontented and frustrated, either with my circumstances or people, I remind myself to be patient because God is faithful to fulfill His promises.

*"I heard the voice from heaven saying, "Write, 'Blessed are the dead who die in the Lord from now on.'" "Yes," says the Spirit, "that they may rest from their labors; for their works follow with them."*

Revelation 14:13 (WEB)

# THE REWARD

## THAT WILL FOLLOW
## CHAPTER 6

*"Blessed are those who hunger and thirst after righteousness, for they shall be filled."*
Matthew 5:6 (WEB)

I have been in this situation before: Just as I am about to pull into the drive-thru to grab a bite to eat, I get sent to call after call after call. By the end of it, I am so hungry that I thought my stomach was going to digest itself. Driving by a restaurant and smelling the pleasing odor of food cooking makes my stomach cry out, "Why are you doing this to me?" Then there are those hot summer days when I find myself standing in the sun working a traffic crash while wearing a hot polyester uniform, duty belt, and bulletproof vest. I get so hot and thirsty that I feel like the call will never end so I can get a drink of water. Just the thought of a refreshing ice cold bottle of water makes the thirstiness seem all the more severe.

Then that moment comes when I am finally able to stop somewhere and grab something to eat or a refreshing drink. This is the physical filling of my body based on my need for food or drink. When Jesus said that those who thirst and hunger for righteousness shall be filled, I figured that He was speaking in a spiritual context. I wanted to know what righteousness was and why I should so eagerly seek it out. Since I didn't figure that it would be cheeseburgers, I also wanted to know what I would be filled with as a result of desiring righteousness.

*"But the fruit of the Spirit is love, joy, peace, patience, kindness, goodness, faithfulness, gentleness, self-control; against such things there is no law."*
Galatians 5:22-23 (NASB)

Righteousness can be described as the goodness of God and it seems logical that I should desire to be good, because God is good. When Jesus said that I would be filled, what did He mean? What would I be filled with? When I became a Christian and accepted Jesus Christ as my Savior, I received the Holy Spirit. The purpose of receiving the Spirit is for Him to work in me and change my life. Those changes are evident by the fruit of the Spirit. When I seek and desire God and His goodness, I begin to display that fruit.

"The fruit of the Holy Spirit is the result of the Holy Spirit's presence in the life of a Christian."[6] As a whole, all of the traits mentioned in Galatians 5:22-23 make up the fruit of the Spirit. One part of that fruit is goodness, which can be viewed as either a character trait (attitude and behavior) or it can be viewed as an action (good works).

*"You are the light of the world. A city located on a hill can't be hidden."*
Matthew 5:14 (WEB)

Through the years, I have found that the overall view of the general public is that police officers are bullies with badges or jerks on power trips. They typically don't want us around unless they need something. That's a rather dim view of those who are called to serve the public. As a Christian, it is my responsibility to shine a beacon of light into that darkness and let my attitude toward others serve as a testimony for righteousness to those around me. I am also able to glorify God when I share my witness through my good works.

*"Even so, let your light shine before men; that they may see your good works, and glorify your Father who is in heaven."*
Matthew 5:16 (WEB)

The eyes of my two children light up when they see me in uniform. To them, I am a super hero on a mission to go "catch the bad guys." I can recall when my son, who was about five years old at the time, asked me if I was going out to catch the bad guys. I told him that I was and he asked me if I was going to tell them about Jesus too. That was one of those "Aha!" moments when I realized that my children are watching me, and they will begin to take on traits of my behavior. My son even gives gospel tracts to the cashier when we check out at a store. With that in mind, I should strive to be a Godly example to my children and family. My children, and wife, should see me put into action the characteristics that represent God. They should see me being loving to others, they should see me be selflessly giving with my money, they should see me be willing to forgive those who have wronged me, and they should see my patience in times of frustration.

In addition to allowing my family to see the characteristics that represent God, as a police officer, I should allow people that I encounter on the job to see those same qualities. The people that I encounter during the course of my duties include coworkers, criminals, family and children of criminals, victims, and the family and children of victims. All of these people should see me being merciful, forgiving, loving, and encouraging. Does this mean that I am all of those things all of the time? No, I'm not. I'm fallible and quite often miss the mark. I do, however, learn from my mistakes and use those opportunities as lessons learned.

An example of this happened one summer afternoon when I was assisting another officer with a traffic stop in a trailer park. Before any backup arrived, one of the occupants of the vehicle, a woman, got out and went inside with a small puppy. A few moments later, she came back out. After the investigating officer talked to the other occupants, he learned that while being pulled over, this female had received some illegal drugs from one of the rear passengers. By the time that I had arrived, he was trying to determine if she had the drugs hidden on her person or if she had taken them inside with the puppy.

We were trying to get this woman to be truthful with us about what she did with the drugs, but she just kept lying. I don't know if you know much about the heat and humidity of a Louisiana summer, but it was oppressively hot outside that day and I was pouring sweat. My frustration with her lies was growing and the heat that my vest was trapping certainly wasn't helping. After questioning this female for about thirty minutes, and even confronting her with the statement that was made by the other passenger about her receiving the drugs, she maintained her story that she didn't have them and didn't know what we were talking about. My patience had finally run out and I told her that she was full of crap, although I didn't say crap. She started crying and told me not to cuss at her.

Through the investigation, we learned that the woman had hidden the drugs in her bra. Since the officer that stopped her was a K-9 unit and I was the only one on scene with a cage, I transported her to the jail. The entire way there, I wanted to witness to her and share with her the gospel, but I just couldn't do it. I felt so ashamed about losing my patience and using profanity with her. All I could think about was, "How am I going to talk about the love of Christ when I just cussed at this lady?" I kick myself for missing out on an opportunity to witness because I let my temper get in the way. If I had the situation to do over again, I would have not let my temper and offensive language get in the way of an opportunity to share the Gospel.

*"But our citizenship is in heaven, from which we also eagerly wait for a savior, the Lord Jesus Christ."*
Philippians 3:20 (HCSB)

For a profession that, at times, does not have a good relationship with the public, we should be the ambassadors of Christ that reflect His light. There is a photograph that I saw floating around the internet some time ago of a Trooper with the Louisiana State Police kneeling in prayer on the side of a highway after a fatal traffic crash that claimed the lives of two children. From looking at a wide angle shot of the scene, it didn't appear that the trooper's actions were intended to be seen by the general public (he was kneeling beside his unit between it and a guard rail), but nonetheless someone was watching and snapped a quick photo. This uniformed trooper's personal response to someone else's tragedy is the type of action that displays the true meaning of being an ambassador to the department and being an ambassador to Christ.

*"Therefore encourage one another and build each other up as you are already doing. "*
1 Thessalonians 5:11 (HCSB)

I recently stopped a lady for a minor traffic violation. Instead of writing her a ticket, I decided to let her go with a warning. I started witnessing to her and found out that she was a born again believer in Jesus Christ. I asked her how often she shared her faith with other people. She said that she tried to do it when she could, but it wasn't something that she did regularly. I told her that it wasn't until recently that I began sharing my faith with others. I gave her a tract booklet that had a website for her to check out so she could get some materials which would teach her how to effectively witness to people. We will talk more about the witnessing materials in a later chapter. All that this lady needed was a little encouragement and a little information to really get her motivated in sharing the Gospel.

> *"We exhort you, brothers, admonish the disorderly, encourage the faint-hearted, support the weak, be patient toward all."*
> 1 Thessalonians 5:14 (WEB)

One day while working traffic enforcement I stopped a lady for doing 42 MPH in a 25 MPH speed zone. While checking her license, I noticed that this lady looked frazzled. I could tell that something wasn't right, so I asked her where she was going. She said that she headed to an assisted living facility to visit her husband who had been in a car crash and nearly died. After receiving physical therapy, he was able to walk, but had limited mobility in his arms. As this sweet lady and I had a spiritual conversation, I learned that she was a born again believer who was going through a rough time. I decided not to write her a ticket and gave her a friendly warning to slow down. As I wished her well, before sending her on her way, she grabbed my hand and gave me a sincere, teary-eyed thank you.

At that moment, I felt the Holy Spirit speaking to me, saying that this woman needed some encouragement. I asked her if she wanted to have prayer and she said that she would greatly appreciate it. So, right there on the side of the road, with traffic passing and the world going by, we had prayer. I prayed for a blessing for her family and for a healing for her husband. I prayed that God would not only draw them closer to Him, but to each other as husband and wife. It doesn't take long to prayerfully speak words of encouragement over someone and their family; we just have to be willing.

*"But collect for yourselves treasures in heaven, where neither moth nor rust destroys, and where thieves don't break in and steal."*
Matthew 6:20 (HCSB)

The average, everyday person may not provide police officers with the recognition or accolades that are due, but God has promised rewards and eternal blessings in Heaven for those who do His will. The general public, my coworkers, or even my supervisors may not see all that I do for God while on duty. They may not see me giving money to a hungry person for a meal, they may not see me being merciful to someone who is struggling financially by giving them a warning instead of a ticket, or they may not see me trying to save someone's soul from an eternity in Hell by witnessing to them and sharing the Gospel of Jesus Christ. It's possible that even if they do see those things being done, they might not care about my good works for the Lord. I can, however, be sure that God sees all that I do and cares about my service to others.

*"So then each one of us will give account of himself to God."*
Romans 14:12 (WEB)

We all have been subpoenaed to court to give our testimony about the facts of a case. We are asked questions by the prosecuting attorney who will have us go into greater detail about the stronger (good) parts of the case, and we are asked questions by the defense attorney who will have us go into greater detail about the weaker (bad) parts of the case. In most cases, the judge hears the facts and then makes a ruling. One day we will take our last breath and we will be accountable to the ultimate judge, God, and we will have to give Him an explanation for everything that we have said and have done – good or bad – during our lives.

*"For God will bring every work into judgment, with every hidden thing, whether it is good, or whether it is evil."*
Ecclesiastes 12:14 (WEB)

This leads into an excellent opportunity to reflect on what you, as a police officer, have done in your life and career. Consider what God will think when you give Him the account of your life. Being a Christian does not mean that you are perfect and free from any sins or wrongdoing. We are fallible and make mistakes, but we are able to repent of our sins and ask for God's forgiveness.

I want to present to God all of the good deeds that I have done in my life. I want to present to Him all of the times that I have given to others, all of the forgiveness and mercy that I have given to others, and all of the times that I witnessed to others. I do not want to present to Him all of the times that I lied, all of the times that I lusted after others, all of the times that I used idle words or profanity and took His name in vain, or all of the times that I selfishly put myself before others. What do YOU want to present to God from your life?

*Now these three remain: faith, hope, and love.*
*But the greatest of these is love.*
1 Corinthians 13:13 (HCSB)

# THE GREATEST

## OF THESE IS LOVE

### CHAPTER 7

*"Blessed is he whose transgression is forgiven, whose sin is covered."*
Psalm 32:1 (KJV)

The initial reaction to seeing a chapter about police officers loving others might produce some sighs, eye rolls, or shakes of the head. You're probably thinking that this chapter is going to be about how "lovey dovey" we should be as cops and that we ought to be holding hands while singing "Kumbayah" with the bad guys instead of locking them up. That's not it at all. Throughout this chapter, I want to convey the importance of loving others with kindness, mercy, and forgiveness, but please remember that when I put on my boots and walk into this world, I see the same evil that you do. Loving those who cause evil isn't always easy because our human mind can't comprehend loving someone who does evil things. Then, there are times when people refuse to be loved. They won't allow someone else to do good things for them. They are holding onto hatred and bitterness.

Being forgiven of my sins by God is a blessing. He didn't have to forgive my sins against Him, but He did. He loves me so much that He sent Jesus to die in my place and pay my penalty. I'm not deserving of His forgiveness, but I'm certainly grateful that He loves me enough to give me His grace. Likewise, we are to extend that same love to our fellow man. I don't know that we can demonstrate sacrificial love to someone else, but we can certainly try. Maybe my sacrifice comes in that I don't want to forgive someone and love them, but I do it anyway.

*"One of the scribes approached. When he heard them debating and saw that Jesus answered them well, he asked Him, "Which command is the most important of all?" "This is the most important," Jesus answered: Listen, Israel! The Lord our God, the Lord is One. Love the Lord your God with all your heart, with all your soul, with all your mind, and with all your strength. "The second is: Love your neighbor as yourself. There is no other command greater than these."*

Mark 12:28-31 (HCSB)

Here in Mark 12, Jesus' two part answer put God's commandment of love into perspective. First, we should love God, our Father, with everything that we have. Second, we are to love others as much as we love ourselves. If we put the love of God and the love of others above all else, we won't break the Ten Commandments. The first four Commandments relate to the love of God, and the last six Commandments relate to the love of our fellow man.

*"not paying back evil for evil or insult for insult but, on the contrary, giving a blessing, since you were called for this, so that you can inherit a blessing."*

1 Peter 3:9 (HCSB)

Whenever we put on the uniform, we instantly become a target for people to do awful things to us. We are cussed, told that we are worthless, hit, and spit on. When those things happen to us, we will likely have natural human anger and emotions, but it's our job as Christians to keep some of our actions in check and act with a forgiving heart. Do you remember in the introduction section how I mentioned that I wrote this book partially to myself as motivation and guidance? Well, we can mark this paragraph down as "note to self."

There was one time when I arrested a young man for an outstanding felony warrant. He continually lied to me about his name, and when I discovered his true identity, he became belligerent. He accused me of racism and said that I was harassing him because of the color of his skin. That wasn't true and I resented the accusation. Throughout my career, whether I was a lost person or a born again Christian, I have been able to hold my head high when it comes to treating people equally, but not this time. I lost my temper with him and said some unprofessional things, mostly in the form of four lettered words. I gave back as good as I got…well, as bad as I got. I didn't obey the instructions in 1 Peter about not repaying insult for insult.

After the bad guy was in jail, I reflected on the situation and how I behaved. I was embarrassed and humiliated that, out of anger, I would sink low enough to pepper this person with cuss words. I'm thankful to know that because I am willing to repent for my actions, God is willing to forgive my anger. I'm a police officer, but at the same time I'm human. I will stumble and fall when it comes to my actions and words, but I have to be willing to pick myself up, turn away from my sin (repent), and keep going. If I don't repent and strive to do better, then all of that anger can build up and become bitterness and hatred.

> "Hatred stirs up conflicts, but love covers all offenses."
> Proverbs 10:12 (HCSB)

Bitterness and hatred will literally tear you down; they will destroy you. In both my professional life and my personal life, I have been bitter, and I have hated. What I gave to others in bitterness and hatred, I received in misery and stress. Being bitter and unforgiving is like shooting yourself and hoping that the other person will die. I thought that it would be much easier to hate someone than to love, but it's actually the opposite. Constantly being bitter about something and hating someone was consuming. It consumed so much time and energy. My life became miserable because I was constantly stressed and I couldn't sleep at night because I was preoccupied with being bitter. I was bitter about personal circumstances, which related to my wife's school and internship, and professional circumstances, which had to do with the stresses of being a police officer. My bitterness and hatred towards others began to wear on my family. I was simply not a nice person to be around.

In the end, I resolved to give all of my bitterness and hatred to God. I became willing to allow Him to deal with the situations rather than being angry. God taught me that I had to be open to learning how to love others.

Living a life of love will reduce stress and make life more enjoyable. God is willing to take the bitterness and hatred, but more importantly, are you willing to let go and give it up?

*"For if you forgive people their wrongdoing, your heavenly*
*Father will forgive you as well."*
Matthew 6:14 (HCSB)

There will be many times in your policing career when someone will say or do something that will hurt you emotionally or physically. Sometimes they will be complainants and suspects, and at other times, they will be your coworkers. I have learned through the years that people do things for reasons that are often unexplained, but I must learn to forgive them. We have all trespassed against God; so in order to receive His forgiveness, we must forgive those who hurt us.

I once received a tongue lashing from a superior officer for something that I didn't do. Arguing with this supervisor would have made things a lot worse. When I left the scene, I was fuming. I was so mad, I could hardly contain myself. I wanted to retaliate by returning the harsh words, but I didn't. Instead, after several weeks, I decided to stop being angry and to forgive this person. Forgiving relieved me of the burden of anger that I'd been carrying. I felt lighter when I let it go and forgave. After that, we continued to have a good working relationship. I'm not saying that forgiveness comes immediately or easily, but in the end, it should come.

I really began to understand forgiveness when I heard a sermon preached about it one Sunday at church. What stood out to me was this: the pastor said that when you forgive someone, you will still remember the wrong that was committed, but when you truly, in your heart, forgive them, you will no longer care that you were wronged. To me, that was powerful! I can forgive someone and still remember what they did, but I no longer care. I still remember the way that the supervisor harshly accused me of something that I didn't do, but since I chose to forgive, I just don't care.

*"And be kind to one another, tender hearted, forgiving each other, just as*
*God also in Christ forgave you."*
Ephesians 4:32 (WEB)

Forgiveness is often the last thing that we want to give to someone who has hurt or wronged us. One night on patrol, I came into contact with a young man on the side of the highway. As we were talking, I could tell that something wasn't right. The guy said that I could search him and as he "assumed the position," he dropped a small bag of marijuana onto the ground. He adamantly denied it was his, despite the fact that I had watched him drop it. My backup and I tried to place him under arrest and he wasn't having it. One heck of a fight started, and as we tried to put handcuffs on the guy, I got kicked and punched several times. We finally got him restrained and took him to jail. My emotions were running high and I was angry that this guy had physically assaulted me. I harbored this anger for a long time, but after becoming a Christian, I was able to forgive him and "let it go". Why would I not forgive him? After all, I want God to forgive me for all of the wrong that I have done to Him, so I will continue to forgive others.

*"Don't seek revenge yourselves, beloved, but give place to God's wrath. For it is written, "Vengeance belongs to me; I will repay, says the Lord."*
Romans 12:19 (WEB)

I've worked in neighborhoods known for retaliatory gang violence. I've found that rather than calling the police, the gang members were trying to avenge themselves or other gang members for "wrongs" that were committed against them. What they should have done was allow the authorities to investigate and bring the offenders to justice. Likewise, we should not try to avenge ourselves, but allow God, the Authority, to bring those who offend against us to justice. I have seen too many times when a young person takes matters into their own hands to retaliate against someone else. It's usually that the one seeking revenge was "disrespected" by the offending party in front of their friends. What happens next is usually a drive-by shooting or a "jumping" where the offender takes a severe beating at the hands of the one seeking revenge.

Whether it is because of some broken bones and the hospital reports the crime or it is one of those times when one of the stray bullets from a drive-by hit a target, at some point, the injuries are going to become so severe that the police will get involved. When we get involved, someone usually gets arrested.

I have to wonder if a 17-year-old sitting in jail for murdering someone because they disrespected them would say that their actions were worth it.

They should let justice take its course. I understand that the "wheels of justice" sometimes seem to turn slowly, but the end result is justice. Just as we should allow the legal system to provide justice, we should allow God to do the same. God will administer fair judgment on those who do not repent of their sins against Him.

*"Blessed are those who have been persecuted for righteousness' sake, for theirs is the Kingdom of Heaven."*
Matthew 5:10 (WEB)

There are different forms of persecution that police officers can face. I have experienced a couple of different types of persecution while performing my duties, one of them being the target of frivolous civil lawsuits and the other being in the form of civilian complaints to my superiors. In one of the civil suits against me, the "plaintiff" said that I violated his civil rights by wrongfully arresting him. He was right in the fact that I arrested him, but I didn't do so until after I got testimony from his three accomplices pointing him out as the mastermind. Oh, did I fail to mention that he also gave me not one, but two confessions. Yeah, that one was quickly dismissed in federal court. I have also been the subject of civilian complaints. After a while, the complaints would get frustrating to deal with, but I had someone tell me once, "If you don't get complained on, you aren't doing your job." I would take the complaints in stride, knowing that I did my job and no basis for the claim would eventually be found.

During your career, it's likely that you either will be or have already been sued in civil court. If you have been wrongfully sued in civil court, then you can understand this section. As I said, I've been sued but throughout the course of each one of the civil actions, I was able to hold my head high and stand firm because I hadn't done anything wrong. I was once even listed as a defendant in a lawsuit, but wasn't on the scene when the alleged civil rights violation happened. During another lawsuit, I was the victim of a slanderous news report. There was a reporter who liked to do a weekly "exposé" on a former sheriff. When the lawsuit against me was filed, the former sheriff was also named as a defendant. When the reporter found this out, she had no problem doing her weekly "news report," but she also felt it necessary to drag me through the mud. Throughout the process, I remained quiet; knowing that God would deliver me. I was cleared of any liability and in the end, the news reporter was fired.

After the civil suits, there are the people who want to file complaints against me. I recently had a man who wanted to complain about me witnessing while on duty, more specifically witnessing to his son. One afternoon, I had a partner riding with me and we stopped a guy and his girlfriend, who were both about 19 years old, for some minor violations. My partner built up enough suspicion and asked to search the car for drugs. While he was searching the car, I started talking to the guy about his eternal destination. He was willing to talk and told me that he was a Christian. After a few minutes, my partner returned to question the guy about some empty baggies, consistent with marijuana packaging, found in the car. The guy said that he didn't know anything about them and that they belonged to his brother. I asked if his brother was a Christian and he said that he wasn't. Out of curiosity, I asked the guy if his girlfriend was a Christian. He said that he didn't think so. After talking for a few minutes, I gave the guy a tract booklet with some information about eternity and salvation. I suggested that he read it, just in case he was throwing out being a Christian to portray himself as a "good guy" because of the paraphernalia. I said that after he read it, he should talk about the things in the book with his brother and girlfriend.

About a week later, I learned from my supervisor that the guy's dad wanted to file a complaint against me. He was upset that I was sharing the Gospel with his son. I had two senior commanding officers suggest that I stop witnessing to people and keep it separate from my job, but they decided to get a final ruling from the Sheriff. I was told by my immediate supervisor that after learning about the complaint, the Sheriff said that I had nothing to worry about and that I should keep doing what I was doing.

I don't know why police officers face so much persecution from the media or the general public. Maybe the media is just looking for a juicy story that will boost ratings. Just like the news reporter who was hurting me because she had it in for the corrupt former Sheriff. Members of the public who look to bring unjustified trouble against officers may be looking for ways to feel better about themselves. The father in the second story wanted to file a complaint against me because I was sharing the good news of Jesus Christ. I don't really know the reason why people do these things, but I do know that if we stand firm in the face of persecution, God will deliver us and in both instances, God delivered me from the persecution of others.

*"You have heard that it was said, Love your neighbor and hate your enemy. But I tell you, love your enemies and pray for those who persecute you, so that you may be sons of your Father in heaven. For He causes His sun to rise on the evil and the good, and sends rain on the righteous and the unrighteous."*
Matthew 5:43-45 (HCSB)

Throughout His ministry, Jesus was spit upon, mocked, and beaten. As I have mentioned earlier, those things will happen to us as police officers, but Jesus experienced them all at once. He forgave us even though we didn't deserve to be forgiven. Jesus loved us so much that he died on the cross for our sins so that we could be forgiven and reconciled with God. How loving and merciful is that?!

*"Blessed are the merciful, for they shall obtain mercy."*
Matthew 5:7 (WEB)

Ah, mercy. I can't begin to count the number of times I've had someone beg and plead for a "break" when I was writing them a ticket or taking them to jail or watched a defendant ask the court for mercy upon sentencing. The most typical excuse that people give for wanting to receive mercy is that, "I'm usually a good person who obeys the law. I just made a mistake." Whether it's at the scene of a traffic stop, appearing before a judge in the courtroom, or standing before God on the day of our judgment, we all want mercy. The question to ask is: Do we deserve it? The answer to that is, "NOPE!"

If God is so gracious and merciful to us, then how do we give that same grace and mercy to others? Maybe the answer to that question can be found in Matthew 7:12 (WEB), "Therefore whatever you desire for men to do to you, you shall also do to them; for this is the law and the prophets."

*"Speak and act as those who will be judged by the law of freedom. For judgment is without mercy to the one who hasn't shown mercy. Mercy triumphs over judgment."*
James 2:12-13 (HCSB)

I have not always shown mercy to people that I have encountered on the streets. I've thought things like, "It's not my problem" or "They did it to themselves" or "I've got enough problems of my own." Although I have had one, if not all, of those thoughts in response to someone else's problem, I have to remember that I should treat them the way that I want to be treated.

Back in my rookie years on patrol, I remember working a traffic enforcement detail. I stopped a guy for a minor traffic offense, and as I conducted my investigation, I wrote him for a laundry list of violations. He was having financial problems and wasn't able to get his affairs in order, but I didn't care because, "Hey, it's not my problem." My attitude was that because the guy was in violation, he got a citation – several of them. At the time, I didn't care what his problems were. Looking back, I think that the reason I wrote him so many tickets was because of over zealousness, as well as the fact that I had a position of power over him, which allowed me to abuse the situation. Was what I did wrong? Legally, no, but I do believe that it was wrong to behave with such disregard for the man's life circumstances. This took place well before I accepted Christ and became a new person. Now that I reflect back on the situation, I ask myself, "How can I go to the throne of God and ask for mercy if I'm not willing to show mercy to others?"

To illustrate the change of heart that God can give someone, I will share another story. Several years later, I stopped a man for running a stop sign. I learned that he had a suspended driver's license, his vehicle registration had expired, and he didn't have any insurance on his car. I asked him why his license was suspended and he told me that he'd gotten some traffic tickets, but before he could pay them, he lost his job. He and his family moved to Louisiana from Texas in hopes of finding employment, but he wasn't having much luck. He had a real sad story, and I felt bad for him and his situation. Don't get me wrong here. I've seen plenty of great actors and actresses on the side of the road telling me how bad their situation was while facing either a traffic ticket or arrest, but every internal alarm that I had was going off telling me, "This person is full of it." In this case I believed that his circumstances were genuine.

You may be wondering if I wrote him a ticket. Well, the answer is that I did. I still have a job to do, but I was merciful in my actions. I only wrote him a ticket for the stop sign violation, because it was a matter of public safety. After running the stop sign, he could have hit another vehicle at the busy intersection. I didn't cite him for the other violations. Had I given him a ticket for the license, registration, and insurance, it would have cost him well over $1,000.00 in fines and court costs, and he wouldn't have been able to get a valid driver's license. These extra citations would have been more hurtful than helpful to this man in his situation. I didn't feel that adding a bunch of extra citations would have served much of a purpose other than to cost him a lot of money, which he didn't have. With him not having the money to pay a bunch of tickets, he would've likely had to serve time in jail, which would have prevented him from seeking and finding employment and from getting his affairs in order.

*"Mankind, He has told you what is good and what it is the Lord requires of you: to act justly, to love faithfulness, and to walk humbly with your God."*

Micah 6:8 (HCSB)

What are the expectations of acting justly? As a servant of God, I am given expectations from Him. I am to seek and do justice, but in doing so, I am to love mercy. God's instruction is that while I do these things, I should humble myself to a close relationship with Him, because after all, He created me. When I look up at the stars on a clear night and see the sky, I'm in awe that the same God who created all of that is willing to have a relationship with me. If that doesn't humble a man, then I'm not sure what will. Everything that I do should glorify Him. As a child of God, it is important for me to have an open line of communication with Him. If I'm open to hearing my Father's voice, then I can serve Him. As a police officer, it's important to have a line of communication with God, seeking His wisdom and guidance in everything I do. I'm constantly listening to His voice as I decide what action is appropriate.

I remember several times hearing God speak to me through the Holy Spirit during traffic stops. I was so set on writing the violator a ticket that I practically got out of the car with my ink pen and ticket book in hand. After getting all of the required documents from the driver, I would walk back to my car and the Holy Spirit would tell me, "Don't write this ticket." I would stubbornly pull out my ticket book, put a citation on the clip board, and get my pen ready because I had made my decision and they were getting a ticket. Here comes the Holy Spirit again saying, "Not today." I just put everything away, give the driver back all of their paperwork, and give them a warning. I tell them to have a nice day, and if the situation is appropriate, I witness to them and share the Gospel. There may be some underlying reason that God doesn't want me to write someone a ticket or even arrest someone. I have to remind myself, it is His plan, not mine. By having an open line of communication with Him, God will direct your path so that you can glorify Him in your actions.

> *"Everyone should look out not only for his own interests,*
> *but also for the interests of others."*
> Philippians 2:4 (HCSB)

If God cares enough to want a personal relationship with me, then why should I not care about others? I don't necessarily have to enter into long-term personal relationships with people I encounter in my profession, but I can certainly care. It is clear that the Bible says I am to look out for myself and my family, but also it also instructs me to look out for others. If I would be concerned about a family member becoming addicted to drugs or alcohol, then I should be concerned for the crack head or meth junkie that I just arrested, the drunk that I locked up for DWI, and the speeder that is doing 100 MPH on the highway. They're not only endangering their own lives, but the lives of others. I would say that those things are definitely something to be concerned about. When we begin to care about someone else, their circumstances become our concern.

> *"Bear one another's burdens, and so fulfill the law of Christ."*
> Galatians 6:2 (WEB)

When bearing someone else's burdens, you are taking their perspective. You see the situation from their point of view. For example, I was called to a residence one night by child services to check the welfare of a little girl. I was instructed that if the child was there, to notify the case worker and she would come remove the child from the home. When I got there, I was greeted by an older, grandfatherly gentleman. I told him why I was there and asked if the child was home. He said that she was and I found her peacefully sleeping on the couch. I notified the case worker that the child was there and that she was fine. I told the grandfather that child services worker was coming to his house to remove the child because of the lack of electricity. This really upset him. He told me that he was a peaceable man and that he had never been in trouble in his life, but if that case worker tried to take his "grand baby" from him, he would be spending some time in jail. He further added a good point about the fact that when he was growing up as a child, his family didn't have electricity.

The more I talked with the grandfather he told me that the child lived with him and he provided for her needs. It was VERY obvious to me that he loved this little girl and that he would do anything and everything to take care of her. I asked why there was no electricity at the house. He told me that he was recently injured while working and that he had been out of work for a while. It was pretty obvious that he had some physical ailment because he walked with a pronounced limp. He also had a disabled wife and he was trying to take care of her. They had allowed someone to live with them in order to help that person out, and the electricity bill was in that person's name. He told me that the person quit paying the bill and the power was turned off. He said that the electric company wanted $500 to have the power restored and he said that he could have the money together in a few weeks, but the electric company was not willing to work out a payment plan with him.

I tried putting myself in his position and seeing the situation from his perspective. In my early days of living by myself, I had fallen behind on bills for one reason or another and had my electricity turned off. I also have a brother who is disabled and after growing up in a household with him, I can understand financial difficulty and the struggles of taking care of someone with a disability. I experienced them first hand.

It was a nice fall evening, and in Louisiana, you can sleep with the windows open and be very comfortable. Well, the case worker was determined to remove the child from the home because the family didn't have electricity. I tried to reason with her and explained that the child appeared to be healthy and that the residence was clean and in order. The case worker didn't budge and said that the child couldn't sleep in a residence without power. My next thought was if a storm came through and knocked out power to the area, was child services going to come through and take away everyone's children because they didn't have electricity? I was eventually able to work out an arrangement between child services and the grandfather where he and the child went to stay with some family members who had electricity so that she would not be placed in foster care.

I really wanted to give this man $500 out of my own pocket so that he could have the power restored, but I didn't have that much money. Well, God never ceases to amaze me. While I was in the middle of working this ordeal, I got a text message from a reserve deputy who wanted to ride with me for

74

a while. After I got finished, I picked him up and began telling him about the case. He told me that his church has a special fund to help out in situations exactly like that one. I was able to give the reserve deputy the man's name and contact information so that they could get his power restored.

*"For you were called to be free, brothers; only don't use this freedom as an opportunity for the flesh, but serve one another through love. For the entire law is fulfilled in one statement: Love your neighbor as yourself."*
Galatians 5:13-14 (HCSB)

The first part of Galatians 6:2 – bear one another's burdens – is quite clear, but what does the second part mean? What is the law? Galatians 5:13 says that through love we can serve one another, and in verse 14, it says that the law is fulfilled in one word – love. "Love your neighbor as yourself," means that I should be just as concerned for others (coworkers or people on the streets), as much as I am concerned for myself. I should be concerned about the troubles of their lives, and I should look for ways that I can help them. Helping someone can be through giving, encouraging, or praying. I should be ready to love, but not judge.

*But when they continued asking him, he looked up and said to them, "He who is without sin among you, let him throw the first stone at her."*
John 8:7 (WEB)

As police officers, we come into contact with many people who are struggling with addictions to alcohol, drugs, or sex; or they may be a combination of some or all of them. We don't know what circumstances brought them to their current situation; therefore, we shouldn't be so quick to judge them for being addicted. I told you in an earlier chapter that I had an addiction to pornography. I struggled with it for years and relapsed several times before finally giving it up. I have never used illegal drugs, but I have used alcohol in excess to numb my senses and escape the troubles of the world around me. I'm human and I've made mistakes. I've made bad choices for a lot of complex reasons, and I bet the same is true for you. What I'm saying is that we should try to understand what causes the addiction, rather than assuming the worst about people. We should try to see them as people, not addicts or criminals, but as people who need a savior.

Being unfulfilled can lead someone to addiction. Being unfulfilled at work may eventually lead to an alcohol addiction, being unfulfilled spiritually may eventually lead to a drug addiction, or being emotionally unfulfilled in a relationship might lead to a sexual or pornography addiction. It is important to remember that addictions don't happen overnight. It's usually a slow fade of morality that brings a person to the doorstep of addiction.

The following story is written by a former drug user who we will call "J.B.":

*"I'm 30 years old and I've had a long journey in life. My father died when I was 12 years old and I started doing terrible in school. I met my children's father at 15 and I thought I was 'in love.' At the age of 16 I dropped out of school. I started using drugs. I tried methamphetamine and I shot up the very first time I used. I was an addict. I used these drugs to cover up any feelings or emotions I could possibly have. At the age of 17, I got pregnant with my first child. During the first 3 months of my pregnancy, I used drugs. When it was confirmed I was pregnant, I stopped. In March of 2001, my baby was born. She was a healthy baby girl. PRAISE GOD!!! This started a whole new thing for me, because when I was released from giving birth to a child, I was prescribed pain medicine, something I had never taken, not knowing this would become my new addiction. I then began using both drugs (methamphetamine and pain pills) at the same time. Just buying dope off the streets was no longer enough for me, so I started cooking drugs, a danger to myself and my child. When my daughter was 2, I got caught cooking drugs at a local store. I spent 9 days in jail, bargaining with God saying, "Please get me out of this, and I will never do drugs again." He did get me out, but I didn't stop getting high or even cooking drugs. This went on for a couple more years until I was introduced to ecstasy. I was instantly addicted!"*

*"When I turned 21, I wanted another baby. I got pregnant, and had another beautiful baby girl. As soon as I had her, I was back at using drugs again. I didn't have a problem or so I thought. I just liked to get high. I started going to Texas to get pain medicine and whatever else I could get my hands on to take and sell. Throughout all of this, I was still with my children's father and I was 'in love again'. All along I was "in love" with any and every drug he would provide. In March of 2007, he left me and my children. I then had to find my own drugs, but I still went to Texas."*

"In July of 2007, my children were left with my sister at the home we were living in. As I was pulling into the driveway at around 6 P.M. on the evening after I had returned from Texas, an ambulance was pulling off. My youngest daughter had drowned. As we were going to the hospital, people were telling me, 'Have faith. Have faith.' Back then, I didn't know who to have faith in. As a child I knew God, but in my addiction He was furthest from my mind. My daughter died and I was angry with God. I did more drugs, went wild, and started drinking. In November of 2007, 4 months after my daughter died, I lost custody of my 6-year-old. She was in foster care and later put with her grandmother. On that same day, my children's father went to prison. We were still not together. He was just a drug supplier. This was God doing for me what I could not do for myself. Getting me away from people (drug dealers) I didn't need to be around. I only wish I could have seen that then. I just went out and found more dealers."

"On January 14, 2011, I went to jail for unauthorized use of a movable (using someone's car without permission). Three months later I was charged with felony theft. This made 5 felonies and I was incarcerated for 10 months. During my incarceration, my sister, who I barely knew, sent me bibles, Christian books, and I only listened to Christian music. I knew then that I need God in every area of my life. On October 14, 2011, I decided that I would 'Let Go and Let God.' I felt the burdens lift from my shoulders and knew I was not alone. I had been to every bottom anyone could have imagined, but I'm living proof, there's never really a bottom. I just kept falling. It never gets better, it only gets worse. I was released to drug court, on October 14th, 2011. Again, that was God."

"I went to church with my sister, and was at the altar. The first officer on the scene of my daughter's accident approached me. I knew then, I was at the right place. I truly belonged at that church. Since I was released, I have regained custody of my, now 12-year-old daughter. GOD IS AWESOME! I have an amazing 8-year-old step daughter, three more step daughters, and an amazing husband. God has been so good to our family and we are truly grateful for all that we have. I've made a lot of mistakes. I've done a lot of wrong. I am so blessed to have a God who loves me for me and knew me before I was in the womb. I don't regret my past. It's what made me who I am today and allowed me to be around the wonderful people I am around today. With God's help, I have been sober over 3 years. I had to go through what I've been through, to get where I am today. It's what gave me a close relationship with God."

My life intertwined with J.B.'s in July of 2007 when I was dispatched to a drowning involving a small child. I was the first officer on the scene and found myself doing CPR on the lifeless body of this precious child. Despite my efforts and those of EMS, she did not survive. As the ambulance was leaving to take the child's body to the hospital, her mother, J.B., showed up on the scene. I learned that J.B. was addicted to crystal methamphetamine and was not present at the time of the drowning. I had a 6 month old baby at home and although I had not been a parent for very long, I couldn't imagine feeling the loss of my child. After J.B.'s daughter was taken to the hospital in the ambulance, I vomited and dry-heaved as a physical reaction to the child drowning, and I lost many nights of sleep over that incident. A few weeks later, I stopped J.B. on a traffic stop and had a "heart to heart" with her about getting off of the drugs and raising her remaining children. I found out that she was later incarcerated and served time in jail.

About two years later, I was in church and the message that our pastor spoke about that morning was on salvation. God brought this mother to my mind, and I began praying for her. I prayed for her salvation and I prayed that she would be freed from her addiction to drugs. I prayed that she would be a mother to her children. I had never prayed like that before. I had never prayed for any of the people that I dealt with at work, complainants or victims, much less a drug addicted parent. This morning was different. God spoke to me and I found the need to pray for J.B.

Well, another year passed by and I caught a glimpse of a woman walking out of the nursery at our church. She looked familiar, but so does everyone else when you work in law enforcement, right? She sat near the front of the sanctuary and as the service went on, I couldn't place where I had seen her before. I asked my wife if she knew who she was and she said that she was the sister of one of the other church members. My wife told me that this woman had recently been saved while in jail and was trying to get her life together. My wife added that she had recently lost her daughter in a "tragic accident." My wife only knew her first name, but when I heard it, I instantly knew that it was J.B., and I was overcome with emotion. As a rush of memories came back to me, I reminded my wife about the drowning incident a few years earlier. My wife knew of the situation and understood my emotional reaction.

After church was over, I approached J.B. and reminded her of who I was. We both broke into tears and gave each other a much needed hug. I told her about praying for her and that not many days had gone by when I didn't think about the day that her daughter died. J.B. is now a regular member of our church! How AMAZING is our God!!! Now, not only do I get to stand with her in church to worship and pray, but because my wife and I aid in the children's ministry at our church, we get to work with and minister to her children. We get to watch them grow spiritually and worship the Lord.

Being able to pray for J.B. and see after effects of her coming to repentance and accepting Jesus as her Savior, was awesome. Being able to share our love of Christ with each other at the same church makes me feel excited that someone else who had suffered an unimaginable loss is now able to experience a peace that surpasses all understanding.

> *"This commandment we have from Him, that he who loves*
> *God should also love his brother."*
> 1 John 4:21 (WEB)

Love isn't always warm and soft. Sometimes, it's cold and hard. Loving someone might actually mean turning your back and letting them face the harsh consequences. I had a family member who spent a decent amount of time in prison. When he was released on parole, he fell back into the same old habits with the same old people. One night, dispatch received a complaint about a vehicle in the ditch. My street crimes unit and I were working the area and I had the feeling that the driver of the vehicle would be intoxicated, so I decided to respond until the patrol shift could arrive. When I got to the scene, I saw the vehicle driving across the road and into the driveway of a drug user that I had arrested in the past. I shined my spotlight onto the vehicle just as the driver popped out. The driver was my family member.

He tried to "play it cool," but I knew that he was messed up. Since his release from prison, he had been spiraling downward into self destruction; however on this night, he was endangering the lives of many others because he was driving while under the influence of drugs. Part of me wanted to let him go, not for his own sake, but for the sake of his child. An arrest would violate his parole, and he would likely spend more time in jail. He had a young daughter who I spent time with and loved. I didn't want her to miss out on more time with her dad. I decided to wait until the patrol guys arrived on the scene, and when they did, I told them of the situation. I told them not to do him any favors because of me; I allowed my family member to face the consequences of his choice. He was subsequently arrested and charged with

Driving While Intoxicated. It was hard to turn my back on a family member, but in loving him, I knew that it was the right thing to do. I knew that in the end, getting arrested would be for his benefit and his daughter wouldn't benefit from an addicted father. I hoped this would be a wake up call, but sadly this wasn't his last trip to prison.

*"A new commandment I give to you, that you love one another. Just as I have loved you, you also love one another. By this everyone will know that you are my disciples, if you have love for one another. "*
John 13:34-35 (WEB)

Children often find themselves, as innocent victims, in bad situations where their parents are arrested; and you are left to clean up the aftermath. When I have to arrest people when their children are present, I make every attempt possible to be discreet and do it out of the sight of the children. However, there have been times when I arrested a parent and their child witnessed the event. Sometimes, parents made things worse by yelling to their child to "see what they (the police) are doing to me."

Within a seven day time period, I was involved in three separate incidents where a child of the offender was present and directly affected by the situation. The first incident came with the arrest of two parents who had violated their probation. They were arrested for selling marijuana and possessing a firearm; both were convicted felons. As we led them out of the house, their child was across the street at a neighbor's house. I could hear the parents telling their child that they would see them in a couple of years. The child is obviously upset and not old enough to understand the situation. A relative took custody of the child, but they didn't help the situation because they were highly agitated and began making an even bigger scene. My flesh wanted so badly to tell the two parents how much of a failure they were and that they did not deserve to have a child. And to the relative who came to pick up the child, I wanted to tell them how worthless I thought they were for escalating the situation.

The second situation was a no-knock search warrant that was served at the house of a local crack cocaine dealer. As everyone entered the residence, I began moving down the hallway with my gun at the ready and I was met by a 10-year-old girl. While we were trying to clear and secure the residence the child started crying; she didn't know whether to get on the floor or get out of the house. After the scene was secured, the girl was escorted from the residence and left in the care of an aunt across the street. By this time, a large crowd had gathered. When the angry mob learned what happened inside of the house, they became angrier. They shouted profanities and made obscene gestures at us. I tried to explain to the aunt and mother, who by this time had arrived, the circumstances of the situation, but they weren't being rational. The mom's attitude was like a roller coaster. One minute she would be calm and I could talk to her. The next minute, she would be just as angry as the crowd and would want to go inside the house while the search was being conducted. The aunt was certainly no help. I could tell that she had been drinking, and the crowd seemed to keep her emotions high. My flesh wanted to immediately arrest everyone for any and all violations that I could and to tell the mom how lousy she was for allowing her daughter to live in a crack house.

The third situation that week came during an undercover methamphetamine drug deal. My team members and I had moved in to secure a residence after an undercover officer purchased methamphetamine from the residents. We were "blacked out" and as the undercover officer was leaving the scene, he told us that one of our suspects had turned onto the street and was approaching the residence. We moved in to detain her, and she became combative. She was physically removed from the vehicle and led away in handcuffs. Her 7-year-old daughter was in the back seat. She was scared and crying hysterically. While other officers were tending to the mother, I tried to calm the girl down by getting on her level and speaking to her in a calm voice. I tried to relate to her by telling her that I had a son that was close to her age. I'm not sure that anything I was doing to calm the child down was working because the mom was getting louder and more agitated. My fleshly reaction was similar to that of the first incident in that I wanted to tell the mom that she didn't deserve to have a child. There are plenty of people in the world who would love to have a child, but aren't able. She was bringing her daughter to a drug deal.

While my head was spinning with my fleshly reactions, my heart ached for each of those children. It ached to know that each of those children had to live in conditions that would cause them to be exposed to illegal drug activity. My heart also ached to know that they are unable to understand the process by which criminals are brought to justice, and they didn't understand that we were trying to make their worlds safer. They only understood that we took away their parents.

Instead of caving to fleshly reactions, I remained calm and professional. I attempted to show the love of Christ by being the example of His love that would be pleasing to Him. I made every attempt to share the Gospel to the violators whenever possible. In addition to sharing the Gospel with the parents, I prayed that God would give the children peace and understanding. I also prayed that He would change the circumstances for the children. I wanted to try to change the child's perception of the police by showing them that we can be loving and compassionate. Knowing that children can be frightened in situations involving the police, I keep several stuffed teddy bears in my car to give to the kids. Giving the bears to children helps to bridge the gap between us and gives them comfort and a better memory of our contact.

*"Let all that you do be done in love."*
1 Corinthians 16:14 (WEB)

In the heat of battle, and the battles will surely come, let love be your guide. The battles that you face, on duty or off, will either be physical, mental/emotional, or spiritual. Physical battles may be the ones that we encounter while trying to arrest a violator. Love them by doing your job appropriately and not abusing your power. Mental and emotional battles may be the ones that come as a result of the stress that we endure from being a police officer. Let love guide you by not being bitter or hateful toward those who cause the stress. Instead, be willing to forgive them. Spiritual battles may come in the form of Satan trying to weaken you to the temptations of this world. Love God more than you love this world. Only God can give true and lasting happiness. That is because He loves us.

I urge you to not let your emotions, anger, or embarrassment be deciding factors for your actions. Let mercy and forgiveness be at the forefront of your mind. Most importantly let love be behind everything that you do. Remember that God is love, and if you are letting love be the guide, then that means that you are letting God be your Guide.

*He told them: "The harvest is abundant, but the workers are few. Therefore, pray to the Lord of the harvest to send out workers into His harvest.*
Luke 10:2 (HCSB)

*"Pray also for me, that the message may be given to me when I open my mouth to make known with boldness the mystery of the gospel. For this I am an ambassador in chains. Pray that I might be bold enough in Him to speak as I should."*

Ephesians 6:19-20 (HCSB)

# CAN I GET

## A WITNESS? CHAPTER 8

*"Blessed are the peacemakers, for they shall be called children of God."*

Matthew 5:9 (WEB)

Police officers are peacemakers in the sense that when we arrive at a scene, our objective is to restore the peace as quickly and safely as possible. I want to challenge you to explore the idea that being a peacemaker not only means making peace between people, but helping people find the peace that can only be found in Jesus Christ. There are countless opportunities to share the gospel with criminals, victims, and even other police officers.

Lost people don't know about the peace and comfort that God can give them when they accept Jesus Christ into their lives. God is the ultimate peacemaker who works within us to calm our emotions when the storms of life rage all around. He can give peace to the parents who lost a child in an accident. He can give peace to a husband and wife whose marriage is failing and falling apart. He can give peace to the person who is struggling with their addictions. It is my job as a peacemaker to share that peace with others and let them know how to find it.

There are times when I've found myself in situations where bad things happened to Christian people. Just because someone has accepted Christ, it doesn't mean that life won't happen. Life around them goes on, and sometimes bad things happen to good people. Occasionally, I have to remind Christian people to lean on and trust in God during those hard times. They have to be reminded that God is the Source for everything in life. He is the God who gives and takes away. When standing with someone in the moment of tragedy, I might not be able to say anything that will give them immediate comfort, but I must not be afraid to remind them that, if they are willing to allow it, God can restore peace in their life.

> *"Then He said to them, "Go into all the world and preach*
> *the gospel to the whole creation."*
> Mark 16:15 (HCSB)

When I became a deputy sheriff, I took an Oath of Office that went like this:

"I, Matthew Hill, do solemnly swear that I will support the constitution and laws of the United States and the constitution and laws of this state and that I will faithfully and impartially discharge and perform all the duties incumbent on me as: Deputy Sheriff of Ouachita Parish according to the best of my ability and understanding, so help me God."

The commission that was given to me by my department gave me the authority to uphold the laws of my jurisdiction and if necessary, take away someone's freedom by arresting them, which is something that shouldn't be taken lightly.

Jesus also gave His disciples a commission, the Great Commission. When we are given a commission by our Savior, it should be taken very seriously and executed to the fullest extent of the Law; which is God's law of love. Christians are given the instruction to share the Gospel with every person. We should be willing to share the truth with everyone, and we definitely should be happy that we live in a country where we can freely do that. Since learning that Christians should evangelize and discovering the ways to lovingly do so, I have been boldly sharing the Gospel of Jesus Christ. I make an effort to do it whenever I can.

In the previous chapter, the importance of mercy was discussed. Scripture says that mercy can be shown to someone by evangelizing to them. "Have mercy on those who doubt; save others by snatching them from the fire; have mercy on others but with fear, hating even the garment defiled by the flesh."

(Jude 1:22-23, HCSB). Mercy should be shown not only to those who are saved, but also to those who are lost; rescuing them from the flames of judgment by sharing the Gospel of Jesus Christ with them. Just as we would reach out and save a drowning person from a lake or save a trapped person in a burning car, we should reach out and save the lost.

I stopped a 30-year-old guy on a traffic stop one afternoon. He was a traveling salesman and away from his wife and two children while on business. During our conversation, I learned that he was a "recreational user" of synthetic marijuana, and I even found some of it and a pipe in his car. After we concluded our business about the contraband, I asked him a simple question: "What do you think happens after you die?" He laughed and told me that he grew up in a church setting and actually played in the praise and worship band. He said that he had fallen away from the church and didn't attend anymore. We had a little more give and take conversation, and he told me that he knew that Jesus was the way to salvation, and that he had not been living his life in a way that would honor God.

I've been through several interview and interrogation training sessions and have gotten pretty good at reading the expressions that people make. I was able to see conviction all over his face. This became more apparent when I asked him if he wanted his children to grow up following the path that he was currently walking. He was holding back tears as I gave him a tract booklet. He told me that he didn't have a Bible with him on the road. I gladly gave him one with an encouraging handshake. As he turned to leave, he stopped and asked, "Why did you tell me all of these things?" My answer to him was, "As a police officer, it is my job to save lives. I might as well save some souls while I'm at it."

*"But I count my life of no value to myself, so that I may finish my course and the ministry I received from the Lord Jesus, to testify to the gospel of God's grace."*
Acts 20:24 (HCSB)

I have come to learn that my spiritual gift is evangelism. I love sharing the Gospel with people and after I learned the appropriate ways to do so, I found that it is quite easy. As police officers, we are constantly in contact with people; therefore we should constantly share the Gospel. You might be thinking,

"Hey Matthew, witnessing might be for you, but I'm not really qualified to do it." There are only two qualifications for sharing the Gospel: you must be born again and you must be breathing.

During the early part of 2012, I found that I met the qualifications, but I didn't have the knowledge. Realizing that I lacked the proper knowledge, I sought after ways to effectively share my faith in Jesus Christ, and I attribute much of that knowledge to Mark Cahill. After reading his books, *One Heartbeat Away* and *One Thing You Can't Do In Heaven*, and watching a few of his video sermons on the internet, I put Mark's teaching into practice. The rest was left up to God. Mark has a lot of great material on his website, www.markcahill.org, not only to help you reach the lost, but to teach you how to get into conversations with people.

Although I won't go into great detail about how to witness, I will share a few tips. I got my start in witnessing by handing out Gospel tracts. These are small cards, about the size of a business card, that share a quick and to the point message. There are endless possibilities to where you can hand out tracts. One of my favorite places to leave tracts is the gas station. Instead of walking into the store to pay with cash, most people will pay at the pump. I will slide a tract in the credit card slot on the pump so that it hangs about halfway out. That way, the next person who comes behind me to pay at the pump has to at least take it out and look at it; hopefully they will read it while pumping the gas. While I'm at the gas station, I can talk to the attendant. I have found that the attendants, especially those who work on the graveyard shift, are willing to engage into conversation.

While on duty, there will be times that the only meal that I get will be from the drive-thru at a fast food restaurant. At these places, there is at least one, if not two opportunities to hand out a tract. I will give a tract to the person who takes my money at the first window and give another one to the person who gives me my food at the second window. For those times when I am fortunate enough to get to sit down and have a meal, I try engaging the server in a conversation about eternity. If they are exceptionally busy and we don't get a chance to talk, I will leave a tract with the tip. When leaving gospel tracts with the tip, I like to really bless the server. What kind of witness would it be to leave a gospel tract and a crappy tip, or no tip at all? Remember that we are trying to show the love of Christ by blessing this person.

*"preach the word; be urgent in season and out of season; reprove, rebuke, and exhort, with all patience and teaching."*

2 Timothy 4:2 (WEB)

I have worked on a street crimes unit where it was my job to make pre-text traffic stops in an effort to uncover other crimes. I would do a lot of witnessing at the conclusion of those traffic stops. I stopped a young man one afternoon for a minor moving violation. I conducted my police business, and determined that there was no criminal activity occurring. I told him that he was free to go, but I asked him if he would mind answering a personal question before he left. He obliged and we got into a good conversation about the cross necklace that was hanging from his neck. He said that he just liked crosses and that he wanted to become a Christian one day. One day? That just took me aback! We talked about the cross at Calvary and what it meant to be a Christian and what he had to do to become one. I told him that he didn't have to wait for "one day" to come around, and that he could get back into his car, repent of his sins, accept Jesus Christ as his Savior, and become a born-again believer. I gave him some Christian literature and wished him well.

There have also been some humorous things that happened while witnessing to people. I was talking to a man one day and we were talking about being good and what God's standard for being good was. I asked him, "You know the Ten Commandments?" In my mind I was asking him if he had ever heard of them, but I guess he thought that I was asking if he could name them. He says that he does and begins to tell me, "Can't kill. Can't steal. The right to bear arms...." Not wanting to offend the guy, I repressed my laughter and politely let him know that "the right to bear arms" was in the Constitution, not the Ten Commandments. After a few minutes, I learned that he'd recently lost a family member and that opened the door for some great conversation about eternity.

Witnessing can even be done when answering complaints. There are plenty of lost people out there and luckily for Christian police officers, they will call for us to come to their houses. They even invite us inside when we get there. It is a win/win situation. We get to help solve their problem and we get to share the Gospel with them.

I also like to witness to people that I arrest and take to jail. Since I work for a sheriff's department, which covers a fairly large area, there is usually a 10-15 minute, and sometimes longer, trip to the jail. I've had some great conversations with the people who were in the back of my unit. I have taken sharing the Gospel to the max by enlarging my favorite Gospel tract and taping it to the glass partition of the cage in my unit. If I get someone who doesn't want to talk, then maybe they will read the message.

There are times, however, when witnessing to an arrestee just won't work. They may have been too high or too drunk or too irate to listen to or even comprehend a conversation. When faced with these situations, I would leave a Gospel tract or some Christian literature with the booking officer so that it could be put into their property. That way, they would have the information when they sobered up or calmed down.

*"but speaking truth in love, we may grow up in all things into him, who is the head, Christ,"*
Ephesians 4:14 (WEB)

I have to remember to pay attention when witnessing to people while in uniform and keep in mind that I'm sharing the Gospel or "good news" of Jesus Christ, which should be done in a loving way. While conducting my police business, I'm obviously in that "police mode." I must have command presence and maintain control of the situation, so I use my "police voice" to direct violators while on the scene, but when I start witnessing to someone, I have to tone down the police mode a bit. I can't lovingly share the Gospel with someone when using my "police voice." The person that I am talking to is just that, a person. Instead of talking "at them", I try talking "with them." I have to be careful of my posture as well. I try to take a relaxed stance, by leaning against the front bumper of my car, to put the person at ease. This seems help them open up with their opinions and facilitate our conversation. In the same breath that I tell you I take a relaxed stance with someone, I will tell you that I don't throw my officer safety out the window. I am mindful of my gun side and keep it guarded. I am also aware of my surroundings by maintaining my situational awareness.

Remember that you are an ambassador, and that you are a representation of our Heavenly Father. Don't be afraid to open your mouth and share the Gospel. It's commanded by Jesus. It's not hard to do and once you are a Christian, you have met half of the requirements needed to witness. Practice sharing your faith, and find the approach that seems to fit your personality. Be bold in sharing your faith!

*For I was hungry and you gave Me something to eat; I was thirsty and you gave Me something to drink; I was a stranger and you took Me in; I was naked and you clothed Me; I was sick and you took care of Me; I was in prison and you visited Me.' "Then the righteous will answer Him, 'Lord, when did we see You hungry and feed You, or thirsty and give You something to drink? When did we see You a stranger and take You in, or without clothes and clothe You? When did we see You sick, or in prison, and visit You?' "And the King will answer them, 'I assure you: Whatever you did for one of the least of these brothers of Mine, you did for Me.'*

Matthew 25:35-40 (HCSB)

*"Remember this: he who sows sparingly will also reap sparingly. He who sows bountifully will also reap bountifully."*

2 Corinthians 9:6 (WEB)

# DON'T BE A SCROOGE

## *CHAPTER 9*

*Be careful that you don't do your charitable giving before men, to be seen by them, or else you have no reward from your Father who is in heaven. Therefore when you do merciful deeds, don't sound a trumpet before yourself, as the hypocrites do in the synagogues and in the streets, that they may get glory from men. Most certainly I tell you, they have received their reward. But when you do merciful deeds, don't let your left hand know what your right hand does, so that your merciful deeds may be in secret, then your Father who sees in secret will reward you openly.*

Matthew 6:1-4 (WEB)

During your tour of duty, you will likely come across people who are in need. You may stop a single mother for a traffic violation only to find out that she needs some gas in her car. Giving her a few extra dollars to fill up might be all she needs to get to make her grocery money go a little farther. There may be a population of people in your area who are homeless. Giving them a hot meal might mean the world to them. I used to carry around "blessing bags" in the trunk of my police car. It was a small tote bag that contained some essentials such as soap, a washcloth, toothpaste, a toothbrush, a package of crackers, a bottle of water, a fresh pair of socks, and a Bible. The possibilities are endless and you can find some great ideas on the internet.

I once had a homeless lady actually turn her nose up at the bag when I tried to give it to her. She asked what was in it and I started listing all of the things. When I got to the part about the socks, she immediately took the bag from me. There is power in a fresh pair of socks! Another time, I gave one of the bags to a man standing on the side of the road and the first thing that he saw was the Bible sticking out of the side pocket. His reaction was like that of a child on Christmas morning. He was elated and readily took the bag because he didn't have a Bible and really wanted one.

> *Let each man give according as he has determined in his heart;*
> *not grudgingly, or under compulsion; for God loves a cheerful giver.*
> 2 Corinthians 9:7 (WEB)

Giving, in particularly money, is something that is often done not so cheerfully. This is especially true when times of financial hardships come. In the early part of 2012, I heard a message about sowing seed where you are fed the Word of God. I had been truly blessed by a particular evangelist and wanted to have him come speak at our church. After talking with my pastor, the arrangements were made to have him come. I told my pastor that my wife and I felt blessed by this person's teaching and we decided to give a $1,000 offering to assist in getting him to come speak at our church. Throughout the year, we began saving for our offering. In November of 2012, my wife's former boss didn't pay her. It's a long story, but in the end, she didn't receive a paycheck for the month. We were counting on this money to help with our offering.

After stressing and praying, my wife and I decided to follow through with our donation and use money that was allocated to other areas. We were able to make our promised offering and since we were faithful, God was also faithful by providing a way for our other financial obligations to be met.

> *"Having gifts differing according to the grace that was given to us, if proph-*
> *ecy, let us prophesy according to the proportion of our faith; or service, let*
> *us give ourselves to service; or he who teaches, to his teaching; or he who*
> *exhorts, to his exhorting: he who gives, let him do it with liberality; he who*
> *rules, with diligence; he who shows mercy, with cheerfulness."*
> Romans 12:6-8 (WEB)

The apostle Paul is talking about serving God with the spiritual gifts that He has given us. Givers should do so freely, leaders should do so with attentiveness, and people who show mercy should do so cheerfully. I am gainfully employed and God provides for my needs, therefore I should be willing to freely give. I am a supervisor at work, so I should be attentive to the needs of my troops. God has given me great mercy, which means that I should cheerfully give mercy to others.

*"Give, and it will be given to you; a good measure—pressed down, shaken together, and running over—will be poured into your lap. For with the measure you use, it will be measured back to you."*
Luke 6:38 (HCSB)

The Bible says to give liberally and that when giving, we can be assured that God will give the increase. I remember once, starting the morning working an overtime detail doing traffic enforcement. I was there because I needed to make extra money to pay some unexpected bills. Giving was the last thing on my mind. I saw a vehicle with really dark tinted windows and decided to stop it. I had the intention of writing a citation for the illegal window tint. As I approached the driver, I discovered that she wasn't the registered owner; she was borrowing her friend's car to take her small child to daycare. After that, she said that she was headed to work, cleaning houses.

I asked for her license, and discovered that it was suspended due to her owing some fees to the DMV for a recent traffic ticket. She told me that she was involved in a traffic accident and she got a ticket. She said that she recently lost her job and was struggling to make ends meet. She did odd jobs to pay the ticket, but hadn't made enough money to pay the DMV fees. By this time, she broke down and began to cry. I quickly realized that she wasn't just crying, but she was giving up. She seemed to give up because of her circumstances. It was like she could never gain enough traction to "get ahead."

I took her identification and the registration papers and headed back to my car. I could still hear her crying while sitting in my car. Amidst her cries, she would shout, "Why?" She was crying out in desperation.

I couldn't bring myself to write her a ticket. I decided that she was going through enough and writing her a ticket for illegal window tint on a vehicle that wasn't hers would have been a little "below the belt." I gave her back her identification, and she thanked me for not writing her a ticket. All the while, I am thinking that I would like to help this lady financially, but all I had in my wallet at the time was a few dollars. Then suddenly I remembered that I brought our checkbook to work that day and I had a brand new $100 bill tucked away in there.

I asked the woman to wait for just a moment and returned to my car. I placed the $100.00 inside of a tract booklet and returned to the woman's vehicle. I handed her the booklet and told her to have a nice day. As I turned to leave, she opened the booklet and saw the money. The water works began all over again. She seemed so grateful for the blessing. As I drove off, she was still sitting in the parking lot, crying. This time, it seemed that the tears were those of relief.

I hadn't started the day with the intentions of giving away $100, especially since I was out there that day to make some extra money, but God moved me to help this woman. Guess what? Those bills that needed to be paid, God took care of me and made a way for them to get paid without any extra financial burden. God is great! If He leads you to give, He will provide the increase.

One afternoon I saw a man walking along the interstate. He was carrying a backpack, and it appeared as though this tattered sack and its contents were probably the only things that he owned. After talking to him, I realized that he was planning to walk 15 miles to the next parish. I knew from previously checking the weather forecast, and by looking at the looming black clouds, that a severe storm was quickly approaching. I gave him a ride and found out that he had not eaten all day. During the trip, I got to witness to him. At his request, I dropped him off at a gas station that happened to be next to a couple of fast food restaurants. I gave him some parting words of encouragement regarding salvation, some Christian literature, and some food money. I can tell someone all day long that Jesus loves them, but if I don't show that love, I can actually drive people away from the cross.

Another way that I can bless others by giving is through random acts of kindness. One morning I was heading to an extra duty detail and I stopped by one of my favorite places to pick up a chicken biscuit. Anyway, I decided to pay for the meal of the person in line behind me. It was only a few dollars, and I asked the cashier if she would tell the person that a Christian man wanted to bless them that morning by paying for their meal. She said that she would do that, and I went on my way.

Here's where the story gets better. About two months later, I go back to my favorite Christian chicken biscuit place, while on my way to another detail. As it happens, the cashier that morning was the same cashier from two months ago. She asked if I was the officer who wanted to bless someone else by paying for their meal. I told her that I was, and she said that she has been waiting for me to come back. Waiting for me? I asked her why and she said that after I paid for the meal of the person behind me, that person decided to pay for the person behind them, and that person decided to pay for the person behind them, and on and on. She told me that one simple act of random kindness passed through about twenty (yes, TWENTY) cars. By the time she finished telling me this, I was holding back my tears of joy. It is amazing how God can use one simple, random act and make it touch so many other people.

Like I mentioned in the introduction of this book, I share these stories of giving not to boast or brag about myself, but I share them to encourage you as a Christian to give and show love to your brothers. I am truly humbled by the blessings that God has given me, and it is through Him, that I am able to give to and serve others.

Giving doesn't have to stop with people that we encounter on the streets. It can be done with coworkers as well. For example, take a coworker to lunch. If they are a Christian, then encourage them in the Lord to share their faith with others. If they are not a born-again believer, it is a great opportunity to share the Gospel with them.

*"In all things I gave you an example, that so laboring you ought to help the weak, and to remember the words of the Lord Jesus, that he himself said, 'It is more blessed to give than to receive.'"*
Acts 20:35 (WEB)

During the latter portion of 2012, I was working an off-duty security detail at one of our local middle schools. This particular school has more than its fair share of kids who come from families who are less than fortunate when it comes to buying Christmas presents. The Lord began to impress upon my heart to do something to help some of the kids. I asked the principal for a few names of students and some of their needs. The partner who I have worked with for most of my career, John Dupree, said that he would be willing to help me out with the venture. Between our own money and some donations we received, we bought Christmas presents for four of the students.

The Lord didn't stop there. My wife had just gotten a handsome Christmas bonus from her new boss. While standing by my car, giving presents to one of the kids, the Lord spoke to me and said, "Your wife just got a bonus. Why can't you give money to this mother to help her with the other children?" I noticed that the middle school student had several other younger siblings. I heard about people receiving a Word from God, and at that point in my life, I was still learning to listen. But that night, God's still, small voice was just as loud and clear as ever. We were able to financially bless the single mother, who happened to be unemployed at the time, and give her some materials on salvation. After leaving that night, I felt that it was truly more blessed to give than to receive.

> *"Little children, we must not love with word or speech,*
> *but with truth and action."*
> 1 John 3:18 (HCSB)

Giving is not always done in the form of money. You can be a blessing to someone by simply giving them a little bit of your time. As I mentioned earlier, I have a disabled brother who has special needs. In his younger years, he played on a baseball team with other people who also had disabilities. It was fun watching these teens and young adults play ball and enjoy the game. Each of the players had a "buddy" assigned to them. The buddy gave them encouragement and assisted them when necessary, but most importantly, they kept their player from getting hit by a line drive or a pop fly. Some of the players could really hit the ball. I was my brother's buddy from time to time, but he eventually stopped playing.

Several years later, as a police officer, I had the opportunity to be a buddy again to some of the players. There were probably thirty police officers that showed up to help out at one of the games. It was great to see the smiles on the players' faces. They got great enjoyment out of knowing that their buddy was a police officer. I have been able to buddy several times since then, and on one occasion, my player told me that he wanted to be a police officer. He was even sporting a plastic badge from the toy store. With the cooperation of the Sheriff, who was also there as a buddy, I "deputized" my player by giving him one of our gold tie-tacs, which looked just like the badge that we wear on duty.

Another way to give to others is by being there when they need someone to listen to them or when they need a shoulder to cry on. Being a police officer means that I will be dispatched to a variety of complaints, but I have found that a lot of them simply involve listening to the complainant. People don't necessarily want any police action; they just need someone to listen to them. Just as Christ is the rock upon which we stand, the police officer will often be the rock for others to lean upon.

I have seen many police officers who didn't want members of the general public to touch them, but there are times when the citizens we serve will quite literally need to lean on us. Those times will most probably come during the time of tragedy, and if they are not surrounded by friends or family members, the responding officer will have to be their support system until someone else arrives. In the meantime, we can comfort them, we can pray for them, and we can show them the love of Christ.

Most often, charitable giving comes in the form of money. It is great being able to financially bless someone else. If money is tight and giving a financial blessing is not possible, then there are other ways of giving to others. Try volunteering with some local charities or simply be there for someone to lean on in a time of tragedy. There are people all around who are in need. Just be open to hearing God and He will speak to you.

*"Blessed is the man who doesn't walk in the counsel of the wicked, nor stand on the path of sinners, nor sit in the seat of scoffers; but his delight is in Yahweh's law. On his law he meditates day and night."*

Psalm 1:1-2 (WEB)

# IT'S OK TO ASK

## CHAPTER 10

*"Everyone therefore who hears these words of mine, and does them, I will liken him to a wise man, who built his house on a rock. The rain came down, the floods came, and the winds blew, and beat on that house; and it didn't fall, for it was founded on the rock. Everyone who hears these words of mine, and doesn't do them will be like a foolish man, who built his house on the sand. The rain came down, the floods came, and the winds blew, and beat on that house; and it fell—and great was its fall."*

Matthew 7:24-27 (WEB)

Throughout my career, I've had people give me all sorts of advice. Some of it was good, some was bad, some was wise, and some was foolish. As a cop, I don't really like to seek advice from other people. Beginning in the police academy, it was programmed into my mind that I have to make decisions, and make them quickly so that I remain in control of the situation. When I don't know what to do in a particular situation, whether it be a call I'm working or a situation in my personal life, I don't want to seek the advice of others because I feel that I'm not in control of the situation. However, the Bible says that it is right for me to seek wise counsel.

*"But the wisdom from above is first pure, then peace-loving, gentle, compli-*
*ant, full of mercy and good fruits, without favoritism and hypocrisy."*
James 3:17 (HCSB)

When I need advice, it's comforting to know that I can turn to God, the highest and most reliable source. The words from God are without blemish; He will not give instruction that is faulty. He won't give direction that is skewed by my social status or how much money I have. As a Christian, I am one of His children, and my Father is not going to give advice that will lead me down the wrong path. I can seek counsel from God through prayer and fasting or by searching out scripture from the Bible, and that is helpful. Sometimes, though, I need counsel from a person wiser than me. I need the comfort of their spiritual guidance, as I seek to hear God's voice.

*"Trust in the Lord with all your heart, and do not rely on your own under-*
*standing; think about Him in all your ways, and*
*He will guide you on the right paths."*
Proverbs 3:5-6 (HCSB)

Not only have I accepted Jesus Christ as my Lord and Savior, but I have also surrendered my life to God. I constantly pray to God and tell Him that my life is His and that He can use me in any way and any place He sees necessary. Although I have made that commitment to God, I have not always trusted that He would take me where He wanted me to go. I was still leaning on my own understanding of situations, which usually left me an emotional mess.

Several years ago, as my wife was nearing the end of her doctoral program, we both believed that we would be forced to move out of state so that she could complete an internship and graduate from the program. This time in our lives was really emotionally painful for both of us, because all of our family ties were rooted in our home town. We were also attending a great church, we had two small children who were attending a great Christian school. I had been with the Sheriff's Office for about 10 years and had worked hard to earn the position as a supervisor. I had so many thoughts racing through my head: where would we live, where would I work, who would help with the kids, and many, many others. One afternoon, while on duty, I was struggling with a pending move out of state and I began asking all of those questions over and over again. I just couldn't wrap my head around the situation. Why would God have us rooted in so many different areas, only to pick us up and drop us in an unknown place? I was driving down the road and out of desperation and frustration, I just cried out, "God! What should I do?"

In the police car that I had at the time there was a small gap, about one inch wide, between my interior light bar and the headliner. Through this tiny space, I could see out of the front windshield. As I lifted my eyes toward heaven, I caught a glimpse of a billboard, and only one word on it was isolated in that small, one inch space. The word was TRUST. The one who understands a matter finds success, and the one who trusts in the Lord will be happy (Proverbs 16:20, HCSB). I had cried out to God for guidance. I desperately needed Him. He gave me an answer that was loud and clear. I needed to trust in Him. During the following months, I would come to find out that we didn't have to move, and God made a way for us to remain in our home town near family and friends. I also didn't have to go through the hassle of finding a new job. My wife was able to do her internship in Shreveport, LA, which was only about 85 miles from where we lived. She was able to graduate and begin working toward obtaining her license so that she could have her own practice. God has opened several doors for her to have many contacts to ensure a successful business. That road has not been easy, or without speed bumps, but God has been faithful to guide us through our journey, because we were continually in communication with Him.

*"Now if any of you lacks wisdom, he should ask God, who gives to all generously and without criticizing, and it will be given to him. But let him ask in faith without doubting. For the doubter is like the surging sea, driven and tossed by the wind."*
James 1:5-6 (HCSB)

As I mentioned in the story about the struggles that I was having with the possibility of having to move, I asked God for guidance and he gave it to me. I was asking in faith, believing that God would give me an answer. I didn't doubt that He would answer; I just did not realize that His answer would come so quickly. I also didn't understand the answer in that moment, but in His time God began to make His plan clearer for us.

*"The sayings of the wise are like goads, and those from masters of collections are like firmly embedded nails. The sayings are given by one Shepherd."*

Ecclesiastes 12:11 (HCSB)

I can also seek counsel from the church staff or my friends. These people are there in times of need. I've had to seek the advice of my Pastor, and he was happy to assist me. During our conversations, he told me some things that, at the time, I didn't want to hear, but I asked for his wisdom and advice, and that is what I got.

Real friends, Christian or not, will tell me the truth. I like to surround myself with people who will be truthful with me when I ask for their opinion. They will tell me things that I need to hear, even if those things may hurt my feelings. Friends don't say these things to be hurtful, but rather they say them because they love me and want what is best for me.

Since I am married, another source for advice and counsel is my spouse. I am, self admittedly, stubborn when I make up my mind to do something, I tend to do just that. It has taken me some time to learn how to ask for advice from my wife. This isn't because she's not intelligent or in any way inferior to me, but because I like to make my own decisions and carry them out. When I am the primary officer on a call, I am responsible for making decisions. As a husband and father, I am the head of my household and I should expect my family to come to me for advice. I am familiar with being in charge and having others come to me for answers, so it took some time for me to learn that there would be times when I needed to seek her wise counsel.

My wife and I have had many conversations where she starts out by saying, "This is probably something you don't want to hear, but ..." I seek her advice because she will often give me a new perspective on a situation that I hadn't previously seen. If you are married, I encourage you to seek the counsel of your spouse. Your marriage is about the two of you being one, and that means doing or saying what is best for each other even when the conversation is painful or uncomfortable for you to hear.

Jesus said that building life on solid Biblical foundations is like being a wise man, but what happens when I need wisdom beyond my own understanding? I can seek wisdom and advice from God through prayer and fasting, as well as the Bible. I can also find honest advice from friends and the church pastoral staff. Since we agreed to be together forever, whether it is good times or bad, my spouse can give me a new perspective on situations, like an outsider looking in, even if what she has to say isn't what I really want to hear. She is there to be truthful. I'm not alone when needing wisdom or advice, I just need to be willing to ask for it.

*"The Lord bless you, and keep you; The Lord make His face shine on you, And be gracious to you; The Lord lift up His countenance on you, And give you peace."*

Numbers 6:24-26 (NASB)

# EPILOGUE

Being a police officer isn't easy. We are tried, tested, and tempted. We are slandered, sued, and generally unwanted when we walk through the door. I've shared my journey with you; not just the high points but also some of my lowest lows. It's painful and difficult to feel the loneliness that comes with our job, especially when we allow that job to consume us. So, we must not allow that to happen. We must rely on God for our fulfillment and our peace. We must seek ways of separating from the harshness and painfulness that is associated with policing.

Law enforcement is a calling by God to a position of authority. Despite being called by God, we are imperfect. We have all seen examples of corrupt police officers or officers who were stressed because of personal or professional circumstances and they reacted badly during trying situations, just as I have at times. Knowing and recognizing the calling may be easy, but living it is tough. It is crucial for us to remember the meekness and boldness of Jesus. It is necessary for us to live out our faith in our every word and action. We must run toward the finish line of this life knowing that in every part of our lives, we have honored God. When we finish our careers, we should be able to look back on many positive memories and be able to say that we served God in both words and actions.

If you are a Christian, then I encourage you to continue to serve God through your duties. I encourage you to take an honest look at your everyday attitude and behavior, and determine if it is consistent with your beliefs. I encourage you to really study the Bible and apply it to your walk with Christ. Be an active participant in your faith, not a bystander. Know your beliefs so that you can serve and protect your community, not just in the physical but also in the spiritual.

Many of the stories I share in this book happened before I accepted Christ. They reflect actions that are embarrassing and painful to remember. You may have been touched by those stories or may have seen yourself in my actions. As you reflect on your own stories and experiences, you may realize that you don't like the person that you are. As you check your heart and conscience, you desire to be different. Jesus can give you a new life, a new start. When you accept Jesus Christ as your Lord and Savior, all of the old things in your life have passed. The Bible says that you are a new creation.

There are many different versions of the "Sinner's Prayer," but there isn't a specific group of words for repentance and salvation. If you want to make the commitment to accept Jesus, then in your own words, you can sincerely admit to Him that you are a sinner, and believe that Jesus Christ died for your sins and was resurrected into Heaven. You must confess that Jesus Christ is your Lord and Savior. If you have done this, then there is a great and joyous celebration in Heaven! I want to encourage you to find a Bible and begin reading it everyday. A good place to start is in the Gospel of John. Also, find a Bible teaching church and start attending. Last, but certainly not least, start sharing what Jesus did for you and how He changed your life. Tell others how they can come to know Christ.

If you have your own stories that you would like to share or simply need someone to talk to, I would love to hear from you. Please feel free to email me at hillms@hotmail.com.

Thank you for your service to your community and your willingness to explore how Christianity might be lived out in your work.

# FOOTNOTES

1.) Beatitudes. (n.d.). Dictionary.com Unabridged. Retrieved July 15, 2014, from Dictionary.com website: http://dictionary.reference.com/browse/Beatitudes

2.) http://en.wikipedia.org/wiki/Beatitudes

3.) http://www.merriam-webster.com/dictionary/avenge

4.) http://www.merriam-webster.com/dictionary/wrath

5.) HELPS Word Studies, copyright © 1987, 2011 by Helps Ministries, Inc., accessed from http://biblehub.com/greek/4239.htm

6.) http://www.gotquestions.org/fruit-of-the-Holy-Spirit.html

# INDEX OF SCRIPTURE REFERENCES

4.) Romans 3:23 (WEB)
5.) Romans 10:13 (HCSB)
6.) 1 Thessalonians 4:17-18 (HCSB)
7.) Revelation 21:4 (WEB)

Chapter 5
1.) Proverbs 16:32 (WEB)
2.) Matthew 5:5 (WEB)
3.) Colossians 3:12 (HCSB)
4.) Romans 12:12 (HCSB)
5.) Psalm 37:7-9 (HCSB)
6.) Proverbs 23:17 (HCSB)

Chapter 6
1.) Revelation 14:13 (WEB)
2.) Matthew 5:6 (WEB)
3.) Galatians 5:22-23 (NASB)
4.) Matthew 5:14 (WEB)
5.) Matthew 5:16 (WEB)
6.) Philippians 3:20 (HCSB)
7.) 1 Thessalonians 5:11 (HCSB)
8.) 1 Thessalonians 5:14 (WEB)
9.) Matthew 6:20 (HCSB)
10.) Romans 14:12 (WEB)
11.) Ecclesiastes 12:14 (WEB)

Chapter 7
1.) 1 Corinthians 13:13 (HCSB)
2.) Psalm 32:1 (KJV)
3.) Mark 12:28-31 (HCSB)
4.) 1 Peter 3:9 (HCSB)
5.) Proverbs 10:12 (HCSB)
6.) Matthew 6:14 (HCSB)
7.) Ephesians 4:32 (WEB)
8.) Romans 12:19 (WEB)
9.) Matthew 5:10 (WEB)
10.) Matthew 5:43-45 (HCSB)
11.) Matthew 5:7 (WEB)
12.) Matthew 7:12 (WEB)
13.) James 2:12-13 (HCSB)
14.) Micah 6:8 (HCSB)

15.) Philippians 2:4 (HCSB)
16.) Galatians 6:2 (WEB)
17.) Galatians 5:13-14 (HCSB)
18.) John 8:7 (WEB)
19.) 1 John 4:21 (WEB)
20.) John 13:34-35 (WEB)
21.) 1 Corinthians 16:14 (WEB)

Chapter 8
1.) Ephesians 6:19-20 (HCSB)
2.) Matthew 5:9 (WEB)
3.) Mark 16:15 (HCSB)
4.) Jude 1:22-23 (HCSB)
5.) Acts 20:24 (HCSB)
6.) 2 Timothy 4:2 (WEB)
7.) Ephesians 4:14 (WEB)

Chapter 9
1.) 2 Corinthians 9:6 (WEB)
2.) Matthew 6:1-4 (WEB)
3.) 2 Corinthians 9:7 (HCSB)
4.) Romans 12:6-8 (WEB)
5.) Luke 6:38 (HCSB)
6.) Acts 20:35 (WEB)
7.) 1 John 3:18 (HCSB)

Chapter 10
1.) Psalm 1:1-2 (WEB)
2.) Matthew 7:24-27 (WEB)
3.) James 3:17 (HCSB)
4.) Proverbs 3:5-6 (HCSB)
5.) Proverbs 16:20 (HCSB)
6.) James 1:5-6 (HCSB)
7.) Ecclesiastes 12:11 (HCSB)

Epilogue
1.) Numbers 6:24-26 (NASB)
2.) 2 Corinthians 5:17 (WEB)

Matthew Hill is a graduate of the University of Louisiana at Monroe. In September of 2001, he answered the professional calling that God placed on his life by becoming a Deputy Sheriff with the Ouachita Parish Sheriff's Office and is currently assigned as a Sergeant in the Uniform Patrol Division.

In 2008, Matthew accepted Jesus Christ as his Lord and Savior, and in 2012, he realized that God placed an even higher calling on his life which was to share the Gospel. Matthew is on the leadership committee for children's ministry and also serves as a deacon at his church.

Matthew spends time witnessing to people that he encounters on the streets in an effort to lead them to Jesus. He also spends his free time handing out Gospel tracts at public events such as football games, concerts, and the local fair.

Matthew makes his home in Ouachita Parish, LA with his wife of 11 years and their two children.

Contact information:
Email: hillms@hotmail.com
Facebook: www.facebook.com/blueattitudes
Web: matthew712ministries.org